STREET GLOSS
BRENT ARMENDINGER

*Featuring poems by
Alejandro Méndez, Mercedes Roffé, Fabián Casas,
Néstor Perlongher, and Diana Bellessi.
Drawings by Alpe Romero.*

the operating system
unsilenced texts print//document

STREET GLOSS

ISBN: 978-1-946031-53-2
Library of Congress Control Number: 2019945087

copyright © 2019 by Brent Armendinger
edited and designed by ELÆ [Lynne DeSilva-Johnson]

is released under a Creative Commons CC-BY-NC-ND (Attribution, Non Commercial, No Derivatives) License: its reproduction is encouraged for those who otherwise could not afford its purchase in the case of academic, personal, and other creative usage from which no profit will accrue.

Complete rules and restrictions are available at:
http://creativecommons.org/licenses/by-nc-nd/3.0/

For additional questions regarding reproduction, quotation, or to request a pdf for review contact operator@theoperatingsystem.org

This text was set in Fonseca, Freight Neo, Garamond, Minion Pro, and OCR-A Standard.

Books from The Operating System are distributed to the trade via Ingram, with additional production by Spencer Printing, in Honesdale, PA, in the USA.

the operating system
www.theoperatingsystem.org
operator@theoperatingsystem.org

STREET GLOSS

CONTENTS

Preface | 9

SLEEPWALKING | 13

Alejandro Méndez: Ciudades- tres | 16

Asolan | 17
Bocina | 18
Sacude | 19
Fiscalía | 20
Scilingo | 21

Cities- three | 22

THE BLUE DREAM AGAINST THE BLUE OF TIME | 23

Mercedes Roffé: Situación para romper un hechizo | 26

Hechizo | 28
Remonta | 29
Umbral | 30
Honda | 31
Nitidez | 32
Delata | 33
Pantalla | 34
Saña | 35
Reguero | 36
Surco | 37
Fracaso | 38
Despídete | 39
Peldaños | 40
Arrancado | 41

Situation to Break a Spell | 42

SO FAR IN THIS RAIN | 44

Fabián Casas: Los ciclos | 48

Verdugo | 49
Pulcro | 50
Señas | 51
Azafata | 52
Galpones | 53
Hallar | 54
Alzada | 55

The Cycles | 56

BREATH, BELLOWED, IN AN EAR UNSEEN | 57

Néstor Perlongher: Vapores | 60

Goteja | 61
Azulejo | 62
Ejo | 63
Rociado, Puntillez | 64
Rocío | 65
Puntilla | 66
Axilas | 67
Bruma | 68
Rozada | 69
Manotazo | 70
Resbalón | 71
Mangas | 72
Fleca | 73
Manuelitas | 74
Entrecortada | 75
Cuadriculan, Cuadran, Culan | 76
Kuleo | 77
Acalambradas | 78
Arrastran | 79
Atrapalhada | 80
Desliza | 81

Madrastral | 82
Trasluce | 83
Gollo | 84
Fólego, Fuellante | 85
Arruga | 86
Azoteas | 87

Steam | 88

WHERE OUR ERROR REPOSES | 89

Diana Bellessi: Lo que se lleva el viento en su rumor | 92

Huellas | 94
Urdir | 95
Esteras | 96
Acune | 97
Otorga | 98
Plusvalía | 99
Orfebrería | 100

What the Wind Carries in Its Rumor | 101

FUTURE SOMATICS TO DO LIST | 105
a love letter to *street gloss*: to brent—jen hofer
Notes | 107
A Conversation with Brent Armendinger | 108
About the Poets | 116
About the Artist | 117
Acknowledgments | 118
About the Author / Translator | 119

PREFACE

I began this project in Buenos Aires in 2011. I was interested in how a poem might be an echo of the city itself. I was interested in the surface area of language and the generative potential of failure in translation. With these ideas in mind, I created a set of procedures to follow the poems of five contemporary Argentinian writers – Alejandro Méndez, Mercedes Roffé, Fabián Casas, Néstor Perlongher, and Diana Bellessi – into the streets of the city.

To begin, I made a rough translation of each poem without a dictionary. I then went looking for the "definitions" of the words I didn't know. I often began in a public plaza or in a place that somehow resonated with the poem itself. For every word I couldn't translate, I made myself walk the number of blocks corresponding to the line in which that word appeared. For example, I would walk five blocks to find the "definition" of a word in the fifth line. At stanza breaks, I made myself change directions. Once I "arrived," I would try to ask a stranger about their own associations with this word, and then take notes about our conversation. I also wrote down raw descriptions of the physical surroundings and my emotional impressions. In this way, the poems pulled me through the streets of Buenos Aires, into unpredictable encounters with the city and its inhabitants. At my desk, I began to collage these notes into a series of poetic definitions, which appear between the original poems in Spanish and my translations.

***

My friend Constanza Svidler, who was born in Buenos Aires, describes the city as a palimpsest, "a somaticizing city, [where] urban spaces display the symptoms of trauma in their incorporation within quotidian life over time." When I walk through Buenos Aires, I feel as though I'm peeling back layers to encounter aspects of the hidden city, as well as the impossible city, a city that resembles Buenos Aires but is, more than anything, language itself: the city that hovers over us. In this book, I have translated myself into a fiction, "my cartographer," in order to translate my own movements. I have made a palimpsest of myself, in order to address the charged dynamics of my relationship, as a citizen of the United States, to Argentina's language, history, and geography.

I was born in 1974, just before the end of the Vietnam War and the beginning of the so-called "Dirty War" in Argentina. Between 1974 and 1983, an estimated 30,000 left-wing activists, trade unionists, students, journalists, and alleged sympathizers were killed or "disappeared" by death squads and the military. As U.S. Secretary of State, Henry Kissinger offered his tacit approval of these actions as part of an anti-communist campaign called Operation Condor. Some of the most notorious generals were trained at the U.S. Army School of the Americas in Fort Benning, Georgia. In 2016, there was widespread protest against President Obama's visit to Argentina, which coincided with the 40th anniversary of the coup that installed the military dictatorship. And today, U.S. hedge-fund investors have a stranglehold on Argentina's economy, and my friends who live there are finding it harder to make ends meet. How is my presence in Buenos Aires haunted by these realities?

***

CARPINCHO

Avenida Santa Fe y Bullrich

It's an animal, the stranger says, the kind that they have up in the delta. A long time ago, he laughs, there was a saying that a kid was a *carpincho* if they neglected to comb their hair. His grandmother used to call him that. A couple walks into the traffic island. The man bears his weight on one crutch, the woman holds the other for him. This choreography of reliance. I take a photograph, the wall covered in graffiti and the iconic grid of faces, copied over and over, bleeding out their definition, the *desaparecidos*, wheatpasted and peeling – a billboard of an underwear advertisement towering above it all. This choreography of ghosts. To see their faces

up close is to see them from a distance. It's winter and almost dusk. My fingers are so cold I can hardly read my own handwriting. Somehow, I mistake the capybara he's describing for a bird. This choreography of accidents. Sometimes its wings can't lift it off the ground.

***

It has taken some time to realize that, like all artwork, this project is not so much "about" its raw materials as it is moving alongside and outward from them. When I am walking in Buenos Aires – how strange but perhaps fitting to use the present tense now that I am back in Los Angeles – I feel that I am walking inside of an idea, but an idea with a very concrete, albeit shifting, materiality. Indeed, I have so many "field notes" that I ultimately had to accept that I would never be able to transcribe them all. The surface area of the city is spreading.

For me, this book is an attempt to bring language back into the precarious space of the body and into the streets from which it rises. Many of my walks took me several hours to complete. There were long moments of waiting, in which I attempted to overcome my shyness in approaching strangers. While a number of people were interested in participating, there were many who hurried past me. Some of them were obviously on their way somewhere, while others were understandably wary of stopping to talk to a stranger. Sometimes, I'd take a break from asking for definitions, and just focus on taking notes.

Eventually, I began to think of the process itself as a platonic form of cruising, filled with unpredictability, vulnerability, and flickering moments of tenderness, as when a man physically kneeled on the ground to show me the meaning of *se arrodilla*, or when a woman touched me in the center of my chest while explaining *restituir*. I started photocopying the poems I was translating and giving them away to strangers, in hopes of creating more reciprocity between us.

What I felt in my body as I attempted this work is only available to the reader as a trace. It is impossible to walk another's path, especially in a different language, without changing where it takes you. I suppose that in this book I have gone so far as to exaggerate this, to make it clear that my translations were never intended to be replicas. They are full of detours, and I hope they show both the delight and struggle of attempting to walk alongside someone else's vocabulary.

SLEEPWALKING

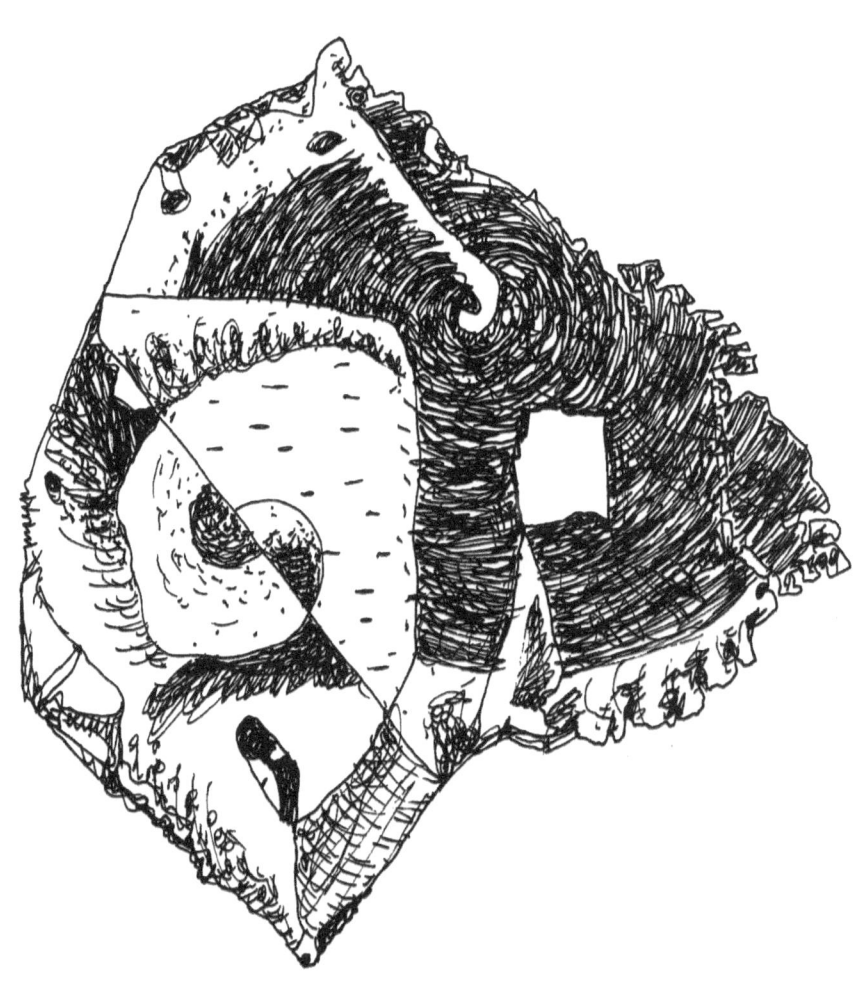

CIUDADES - TRES

Entre personas desconocidas, trajino las calles de esta ciudad. Sonámbulo, a años luz de la experiencia superlativa de niño-luciérnaga, no respondo a los miles de *ring-tones* que asolan el espacio público.

Sólo el humo amenazante, en un piso 20, y la bocina demencial de los bomberos sacude la inercia hipnótica de este lunes intrascendente.

Zeitgeist: el diario anuncia que en San Francisco comenzó una campana de acción *queer* para baños de género neutro. La fiscalía española pide 9.138 años de prisión para Scilingo, por los vuelos de la muerte.

Detrás de mi puerta: una pila de boletas de impuestos, la heladera vacía y cada cosa en su sitio, inmóvil.

Alejandro Méndez

ASOLAN

Catamarca y Belgrano

"Without sun," said the young man, "it means there is no sun," and then he held out his hand, as if for me but not. A word was caught inside a semicolon between *to devastate* and *to plague*. I thought he might point to something for me – he had that face of slowly melting snow – but he only used his hand to flag down a bus. The first symptom was a spool of thread at dawn, unraveling behind me as I walked back to my apartment. In that city, I learned to paste my words to one another – *call me* – solicitation sewn to the body of he who waits for a reply, a thousand paper rectangles – *llámame* – flapping up and down the crumbling wall. My thread, they hung it between their houses, plucking it nightly from small openings inside their barricaded doors. Didn't everyone want to be contagious, to feel the body opening, again again again?

BOCINA

Catamarca y México

As I am writing this, an older woman with a bandage on her cheek walks backwards into her garage until not even her shadow acknowledges me. An ambulance howls and carries its unrepentant howling away, deeper into a city that's on the other side of memory, a dark alley I fumble through when lost, blocks and blocks from where the power lines hang vertically, like unwashed strands of hair. A man presses his fist inside his palm to show me what it means, the smell of detergent so thick on him, it's the sound it makes, the car, when you hit the wheel like this. Each word replaces a warning I cannot hear, unrepentant cargo in the neighborhood of mind.

SACUDE

Catamarca e Independencia

You have to push really hard to make things move, she says, to not get bored, or to deal with the feelings. Her language buckles the definite article to sensation. Etymologically, an emotion is an arrow pointing outward. But what of the arrows inside the atmosphere? From the roof of a nearby apartment building, a cellular tower rises. My consciousness gets heavy, coated with burnt parts of meteorite, unspoken thoughts, pollen, hair, and conversations fallen out of orbit. What if the feelings I call my own have fallen upon me, like particles of dust? My loneliness has a diameter of less than 500 micrometers. I walk, susceptible to the uneven ground of my invention, where the roots of a tree are breaking pavement, pushing so hard to unbelong here.

FISCALÍA

Estados Unidos y Alberti

The dead part of the tree, the brown foliage curled an almost imperceptible yellow, is borne by the still-living branches. The young girl says it's something legal but she's not exactly sure. A woman is making her way up and down the sidewalk with her turquoise broom, careful not to disturb the pigeons. It seems like they ask the right kinds of questions. She shakes it free of dust while talking to her neighbor, as if talking were a means of shaking off what gathers, as if death or dust were something blooming from its bough.

SCILINGO

Laguna Nimez

I walked slowly, and the wind came across the water so urgently in its slowness, so sure of itself it could be nothing less than animal. His name was unknown to me, and because it was and is a name I did not stop. Instead, I opened the window, where I could ask my question without anyone looking back at me. They sentenced him to 21 years for each of 30 prisoners, although it's said he won't serve more than 30. But no calculus returns a name that is not his name, drugged and falling from a hole in the sky forever. An airplane forever becoming the cargo forever inside it. I photographed a bird in mid-flight. The names broken in wrong velocity broken and leaking into the ground. Does some version of that bird hang in the air forever now? The quietness, in which everything speaks to me except for me. When its flying self crosses its forever self, can it feel something, like a record skipping inside?

CITIES - THREE

Between unknown persons, I rush about the streets of this city. I am sleepwalking, light years away from the superlative experience of firefly-boy, taking no account of the thousands of ring-tones that lay waste to public space.

Only the menacing smoke, on the 20th floor, and the demented siren of the firefighters shakes the hypnotic inertia of this unimportant Monday.

Zeitgeist: the daily paper announces that San Francisco began a queer action campaign for gender-neutral bathrooms. The Spanish prosecutor asks for 9,138 years of prison for Scilingo, for the death flights.

Behind my door: a pile of tax bills, the empty refrigerator and each thing in its place, unmoving.

Alejandro Méndez

THE BLUE DREAM AGAINST THE BLUE OF TIME

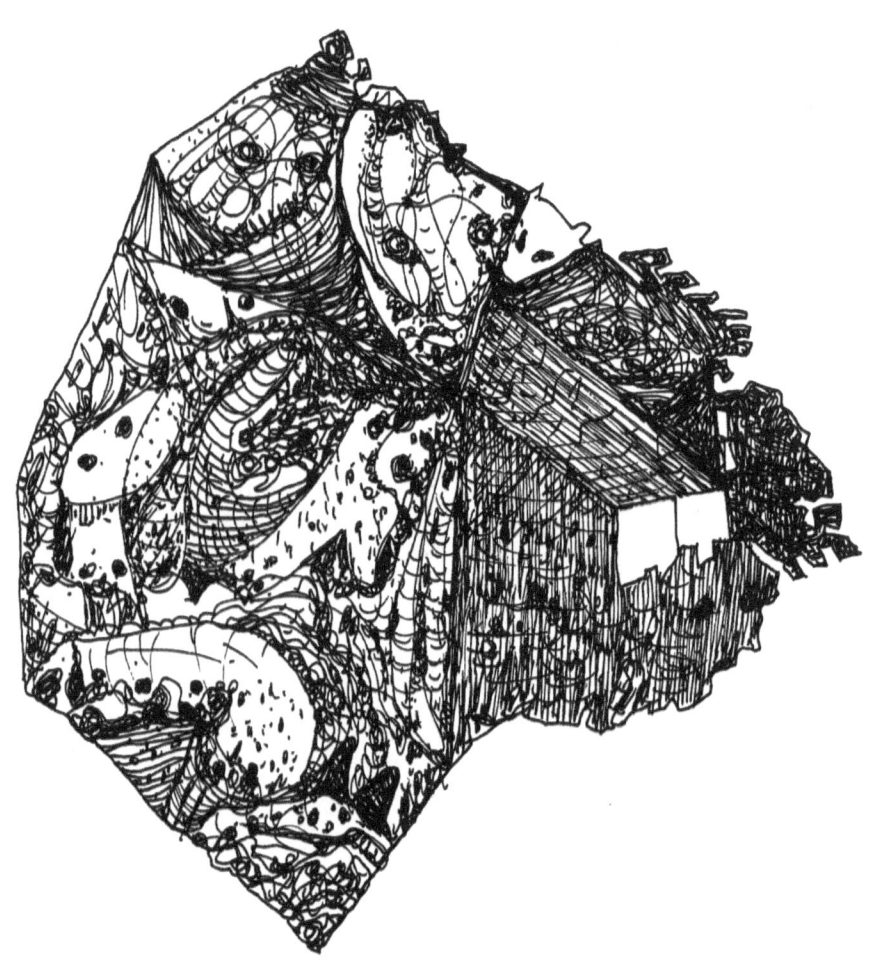

SITUATIÓN PARA ROMPER UN HECHIZO

Acuéstate
      –boca arriba
como si fueras a morir
o a darte a luz.

Remonta
la cuesta de los años
en lo oscuro.

Llega al umbral
      traspásalo / sumérgete
en la honda, estrecha, escala del olvido.

Dime qué ves.
Enfréntalo / enfréntate
a quien eras antes aun de la memoria.

¿Te reconoces?
Continúa.
Sí, reconoces ahora el camino
que te ha traído hasta aquí.
Su nitidez lo delata
   –un sueño azul que se proyecta en la pantalla azul del tiempo
   y va cobrando sentido.

¿Te ves?
Pregúntale por qué y acéptala
–cualquiera sea la respuesta

–He venido a decirte adiós –responde.
No digas más que eso
sin saña
sin violencia
sin rencor alguno.

Intentará retenerte
volver a responder lo que ya sabes
lo que ya le has oído
quizás de otra manera.

Baja los ojos y crea
—con la mirada solo—
un reguero en el suelo
—un surco de tierra húmeda y cenizas.

Verás alzarse un fuego
una pared de fuego
—un fuego frío—
entre tú y tu fracaso.
Despídete.
Dale la espalda.
Vuelve a tomar el camino
—el mismo:
el sueño azul sobre el azul del tiempo.

Remonta los peldaños de la escala honda, estrecha.
Llega al umbral
traspásalo y desciende
la pendiente oscura de los años.

Vuelve a tu cuerpo
¿sientes? —un dolor en el vientre o en el pecho
como si algo de ti te hubiese sido arrancado
te anuncia que has vencido.

El dolor se irá
tú quedarás contigo.

(La memoria del hueco
te seguirá adonde vayas.)

Mercedes Roffé

HECHIZO

Paseo Colón y Cochabamba

My friend told me about this place, the night half-excavated underneath the *autopista*. The guidebook does not mention it. He's in his studio, painting a boy he knows, the curse or spell of beauty. He waits for the face to dry and then paints over it with white. I hold a brush in my outstretched arm, a mirror or a magnifying glass. The guidebook falls asleep. I ask each passerby to pass it over me, until I'm gone enough. The paper bodies of the detained begin to climb the beams. What holds the traffic in place? There is no cover from the sound of it, the smell of diesel, the vibration of these passages. The light shocks them out of shadows and glues them to the wall. They are photocopies of photocopies. An officer is here to guard them. I ask him what it means. In his orange vest, he sways back and forth on the ground beneath his definition. It has something to do with magic, he says, like to get a girl to fall in love with you. There is a softness in his throat, but I sway on the uniform beneath his uniform, the half-excavated night. There is no cover from the sound of them, the curse or spell, plastered on the wall.

REMONTA

Perú y Cochabamba

A mouth opens in the concrete. I think of the rubble behind its grid of metal teeth, the words formed before they are spoken, the heaviness in direct proportion to the waiting. I want to give my gravity away. I ask a stranger what it means. It's to put yourself up on something, he says, like a bicycle or a horse. I think of him, up there on his infinitive, throwing away the clocks and pronouns, covering the sidewalk like confetti. In the beginning, the first person climbed on top of the second hand. I think of this when I am alone at night. It is the only thing that keeps me from floating to the ceiling. He walks a few feet away and stops to look at me – in fact he is dismounting – in order to be here, as if the street unzipped itself.

UMBRAL

Humberto Primero y Bolivar

She knows the sound but not the definition – maybe it's a wall, like this one, covered in graffiti, the opposite of how to tell me. I run my hands over her shadow, hoping my skin will hear something. I want to stand all day, here against this wall, until someone offers to take my place. The color behind our stillness will change. Our collective refusal will be a painting. I want to stand against my scrawling, my ever almost happening. I want to throw it, this how, up against the wall, until it breaks, until it's not a poem anymore. An older man walks by and I ask him what it means. He points to the flat rectangle of marble, chipped in the left hand corner, at the entry of a door. How can a door about to be written or erased be the same thing as graffiti? I want to walk through the hole inside the scratching, the aerosol. I want to walk through the blown-up photograph of a boy, his naked torso. A paper diamond, as if released only seconds ago, floats just above his howling. I want to stand inside the moment right before it leaves his lip, but I cannot get a foothold.

HONDA

Humberto Primero y Balcarce

On the face of the no longer *patronato*, the word for childhood is covered with weeds. In the broken window hangs a photograph of ice. The elsewhere of a continent, a translucent advertisement. The word for Antarctica is Antarctica. It swings back and forth in the aftermath of glass. They say photography is the coldest continent, but I can tell that people are squatting here. Their clothing illuminates the string between the empty buildings. I pluck it with my question. A woman walks by and answers me with homophones. It's a motorbike, she tells me, or that you and I, as if she knows me, we have good energy between us. Across the street is the Registro Nacional de las Personas. I empty my pockets in search of the breath of former inhabitants. A person is a string between the homophones. A person is a continent at the bottom of a continent, a window at the bottom of a window, broken from a name.

NITIDEZ

Av Independencia y Perú

What does it mean to walk between one word and another without stopping? The words I seem to know are see-through. Their letters fall from the dictionary, disappearing before they hit the sidewalk. Clarity, a stranger tells me – *bien claro* – and then what it's not – *oscuro* – and some in-between word I do not know. Perhaps darkness is umbilical, perhaps forgetting is the first ingredient of memory. I am always looking across the street to see the ground where I am standing, as if the traffic were a camera in reverse. I want to see my body disappearing before it hits the photograph. There is a ghost falling out of the parking lot. Perhaps forgetting is the first architect. A fragment of continuous brick, a bruise that outlives the body. The color falls out of paint, leaving just the signature, Grupo Muralista del Oeste. There is evidence of circular scraping on the furthest wall, now exposed to the day. A tree grows out of its center, some in-between word, an umbilical cord.

DELATA

Av Independencia y Perú

When tree is moving imperceptibly, tree appears to be tree. It presses into, and then disappears from, the wall outside this *gomería*. If I am still enough, I can see the names of the previous shops, paint beneath the paint. A worker steps out to light a cigarette. I tug on the smoke between us. It rises to the strips of cloth above me – just now I notice them, tied around the branches. How easy it would be to miss them. Who put them here, the names and ages of who and why?

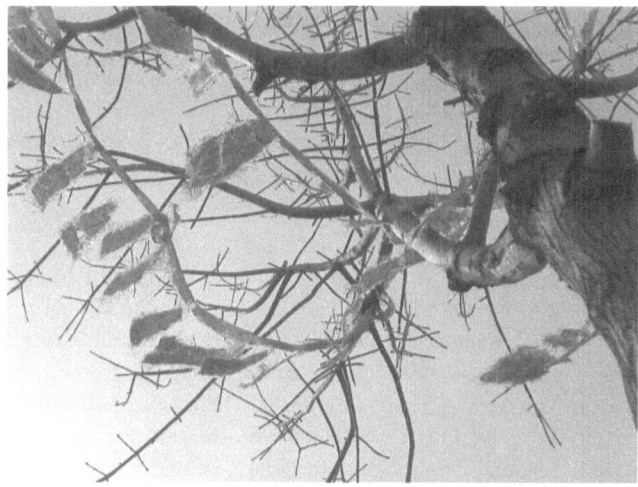

How like leaves they are, translucent, written on the day. A young man smiles and stops for me. I put the word inside his hand. Before he unfolds it, he asks my name. I appears to be I. Is my question a plea to be a name, evaporating in his hand? The sky inside the tree begins to shake. He tells me it's an intervention. When the light is slow enough, it strikes me as a kind of writing. He says it refers to a truth that's hidden, for example, something political. The names continue to shake. Back in my country, an activist stands up inside the Senate: "178 children killed by drones in Pakistan. And Mr. Brennan, if you don't know who they are, I have a list. I have a list with all the names and the ages." The sky unfolds its loneliness and sends it off to hover. It catches fire from the inside.

PANTALLA

Av Independencia y Chacabuco

He puts his hands in front of his face, the little square he draws with his thumbs and index fingers, as if he is holding up the air, the us that floats between him and me. Us is not the sum of singular pronouns, only the between. The L of his left hand and its backwards brother seem to bow, and I think, which one of us is me? Closer than touching is the gap in which a word goes. If I were to actually look inside it, would I see the sound it makes? Accidentally, I give him two copies of this door I am trying to make out of someone else's window. He returns with the extra one and what is the difference between translation and a screen. I put my hands where his had been. I lean my back against his before. I bow my head and the cracks in concrete appear to me as chlorophyll, a photograph holding its breath inside a tree.

The pigeons are still enough to be my shadow. It is winter here, after all, even if I am elsewhere. In what I call my elsewhere, I lean my back against the present tense, a season and its backwards brother. I want to tell you, dear reader, I get lost and lost inside the screen, inside the never ending elsewhere, but the truth is, I cannot enter it. There is no one here to hold it still for me. There is only the machine, and the tracelessness of the air between the pronouns. My cartographer says I should invite you to come and live with me. I can hold my breath, I can bow my head, I can be still enough to be your shadow. Closer than touching is the gap in which a word goes. I want to close my eyes and tell you this as you type it into my computer. I want to turn off the light so you unscrew the bulb and put it in my hand. I want to hold it there until it stops burning, the us that floats between us.

SAÑA

Av 9 de Julio y México

The seeds of the palo borracho fall through the notwithstanding winter. What is it to be prior? Like a tuft of fur, my friend who taught me how to say so. In the photograph, he is pointing to the tree in the park that autocorrect keeps turning into "lash eras." I see him sometimes, a little green pulse on the screen, how to say so falling through the continent. I walk on cobblestones. They cover the former rails, where loneliness continues to dress up as the word I can't define. Soon I will come upon the past tense. This is the lash era, the widest avenue in the world. How could this be fury? The out of place falls through the fact of me.

REGUERO

Av Independencia y Solís

It's not a word, he tells me, so I push it back against the roof of my mouth. His face is a question I have rehearsed and repeated. I reach into my pocket for the poem and he unfolds it, still wet and fluttering, in his hands. He says his name is Nicolás, and then, *do you like to read?* Maybe it all comes down to this. A name leads one question to another, or the pattern of these bricks, an imprint that is not a word. It's something on the ground but he doesn't know for sure. Maybe it is this, an unmarked path between the tongue and paper. I cross the street to where the sun can warm me. The woman begging on the sidewalk and the blank pieces of paper, still wet and fluttering, in her hand. Currency, the little erasure that is not the sun. My face is a question she has rehearsed. I reach into my pocket, but not until I am through with my translation. I take it, the unmarked path between us, and let it dissolve inside my mouth.

SURCO

Av Independencia y Av Entre Ríos

In my notebook I write *young woman – a mark*. Who slides across the hyphen? She says that's what it means, and here I crank the clock into a corridor I can walk through, hands against the condensation on the wall. I ask her what kind. Like a mark on the road, a path, she says, pointing to the ground. Sometimes I feel that this city is written in invisible ink. How can I walk inside it if I go? I won't remember the ground between us, only that it sinks and sinks until we can stand on it. At my desk, it spreads inside me. Like a lover, I beg and beg the mark to leave a mark on me, a groove, erasing me with sweat and teeth. A word floats on top of a word until the road becomes an alphabet. How can I land on what happens when I go? I take a photograph of a telephone pole, painted sickly green, the twine around it holding nothing but rust. I stick out my tongue and taste it, my translation, coming through.

FRACASO

Combate de los Pozos y Humberto 1°

When do all the things I discard become the street that holds me? There's a strike going on. One summer vacation, I brought home a documentary for my father about his union, but I never set foot in the factory where he worked. When does the body become the body? I walk down the street, removing one piece of clothing at a time. My cartographer walks just a few feet ahead of me, and he gives me his coat when I am finally naked. I would like to choreograph this performance, the city through us moving through it in this way. I would like to walk the city from end to end, exchanging what is fleeting with every willing stranger.

I know what you're going to say. Ever since the invention of the microscope, human touch began to flare. Still, my love for visible geometry, like the metal scaffolding holding up this billboard from the backside. More tender and ambiguous than advertisement or warning. A handsome boy approaches, his hands in his pockets, singing, or speaking to himself. When I ask him what it means, he offers me a sentence: *Hoy fracasé en arreglar el auto*. He says he can't concretize it, he cannot find a synonym, it's not poetry but... and then his voice trails off beyond the edges of my memory. What is mine is failure unless it is briefly. At the bus stop, two people get off as if there is no synonym, a choreography from different doors.

DESPÍDETE

Combate de los Pozos y San Juan

I ask the cartonero what it means and he breaks the excess syllables into *chau*. What is the difference between goodbye and the instruction to say so? We carry our life around in a cardboard box that we empty again and again. It has this name – say goodbye – before we even fill it. *Chau*, a variant of the Italian, coils around the word for slave, *schiavo*. Not go with God but I am yours, forcibly. I walk toward the underpass, where pigeons flutter in their small round cages beside a makeshift tent. My cartographer frees them in the night and brings me their cages. Here I am, tossing my words into the metal hollows, trying to remember the shape of wings.

PELDAÑOS

Pavón y Sarandí

On the concrete slab in front of the gate: *Nadie es capaz no pueden cobrar mis recuerdos.* The roots of the tree tilt the sidewalk, pushing grief's white letters to the surface. *Nobody is capable* and then a vine eats away at the barbed wire fence. Nature multiplies the No: *they cannot claim my memories.* A boy from this housing project died in January. I take a photograph of the mural, his arm stretching towards me, thumbs up, his eyes open but somehow looking back into the wall. He was not yet twenty-one. Nobody is capable. Part of his face unpainted, as if the masonry contains him. The garbage strike is still going on, and everywhere the sun gets stuck in plastic. When I reach the intersection, there's a furniture repair shop, chairs stacked upside down. A man steps out and I ask him what it means. He says it's something that comes out of the wall, and he runs his fingers across the moulding. I'm trying to think of how to climb a stair for which there is no railing. The little cave where dust collects, the memory.

ARRANCADO

Subterráneo Línea E, Estación Pichincha

Below the pageantry of history, people try to make a living. They will put a question mark in your hand. It will likely be made of plastic. If you refuse it, you must feel the weight of all the hands that held and did not keep it. As the train jerks its way through the tunnel, a woman is tearing her medical condition into small pieces of paper. Into my hands, her otherwise geography, she places not her body but the splinter. I hold it, the fire of uncontrollably, a single piece of paper. Her doctor has signed a statement, affirming, on the opposite side, the pain of wrong division. What is a body if not a collection of the strangers who are torn from us? I am thinking of Felix Gonzales-Torres' portrait of his lover, Ross, an installation composed of 175 pounds of candy. I take the candy in my mouth, the fact of his weight diminishing. I hold the cellophane wrapper in my hands. I look through it. What is a body if not a broken window?

SITUATION TO BREAK A SPELL

Lie down
        –facing up
as if you were going to die
or give birth to yourself.

Ascend
the slope of the years
in the dark.

Arrive at the threshold
        pass through it / submerge yourself
in the deep, narrow, stairway of oblivion.

Tell me what you see.
Confront it / confront
who you were even before memory.

Do you recognize yourself?
Continue.
Yes, now you recognize the road
that has brought you here.
Its clarity reveals it
    –a blue dream that is projected on the blue screen of time
    and begins making sense.

Do you see yourself?
Ask why and accept it
–whatever the answer is

–I have come to say goodbye to you –respond.
Don't say more than this
without fury
without violence
without any rancor.

It will try to make you stay
to answer once again what you already know
what you have already heard it say
perhaps in another way.

Lower your eyes and create
—with the gaze only—
a path on the ground
—a groove of wet earth and ash.

You will see a fire rising
a wall of fire
—a cold fire—
between you and your failure.
Say goodbye.
Turn your back to it.
Resume the road
—the same:
the blue dream against the blue of time.

Ascend the steps of the deep, narrow stairway.
Arrive at the threshold
pass through it and descend
the dark slope of the years.

Return to your body
do you feel it? —a pain in your womb or in your chest
as if something of yourself has been torn from you
alerts you that you have beaten it.

The pain will go
you will remain with yourself.

(The memory of the hollow
will follow you wherever you go.)

Mercedes Roffé

SO FAR IN THIS RAIN

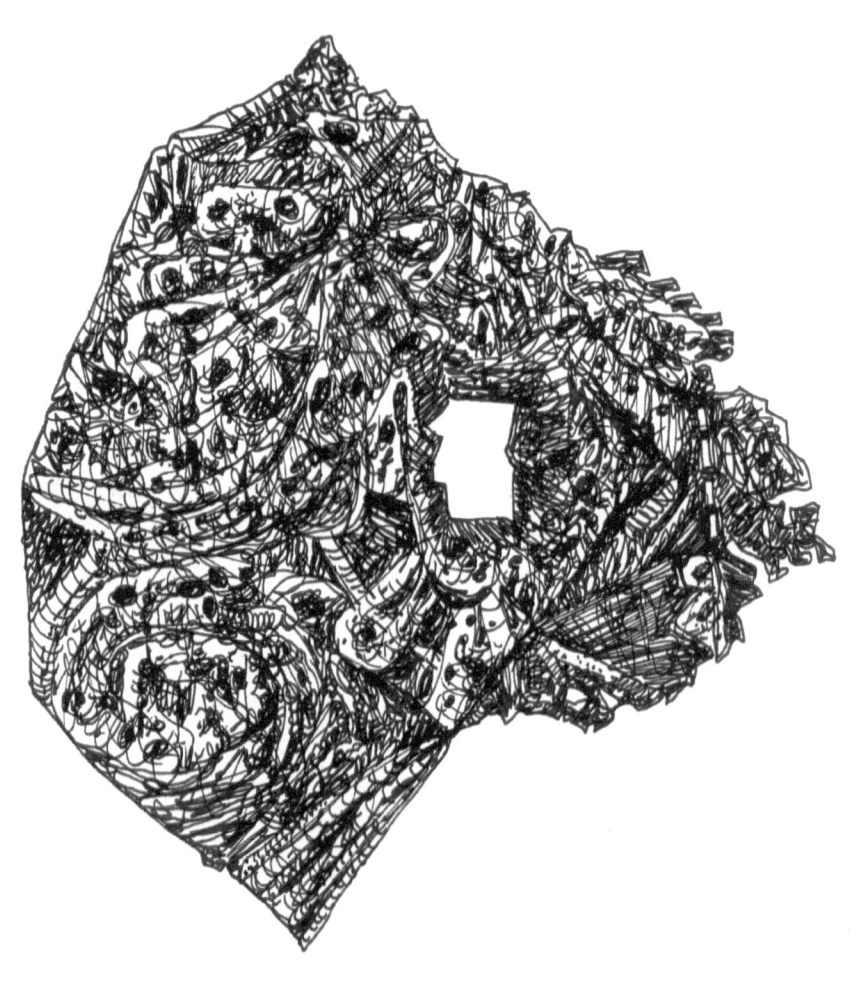

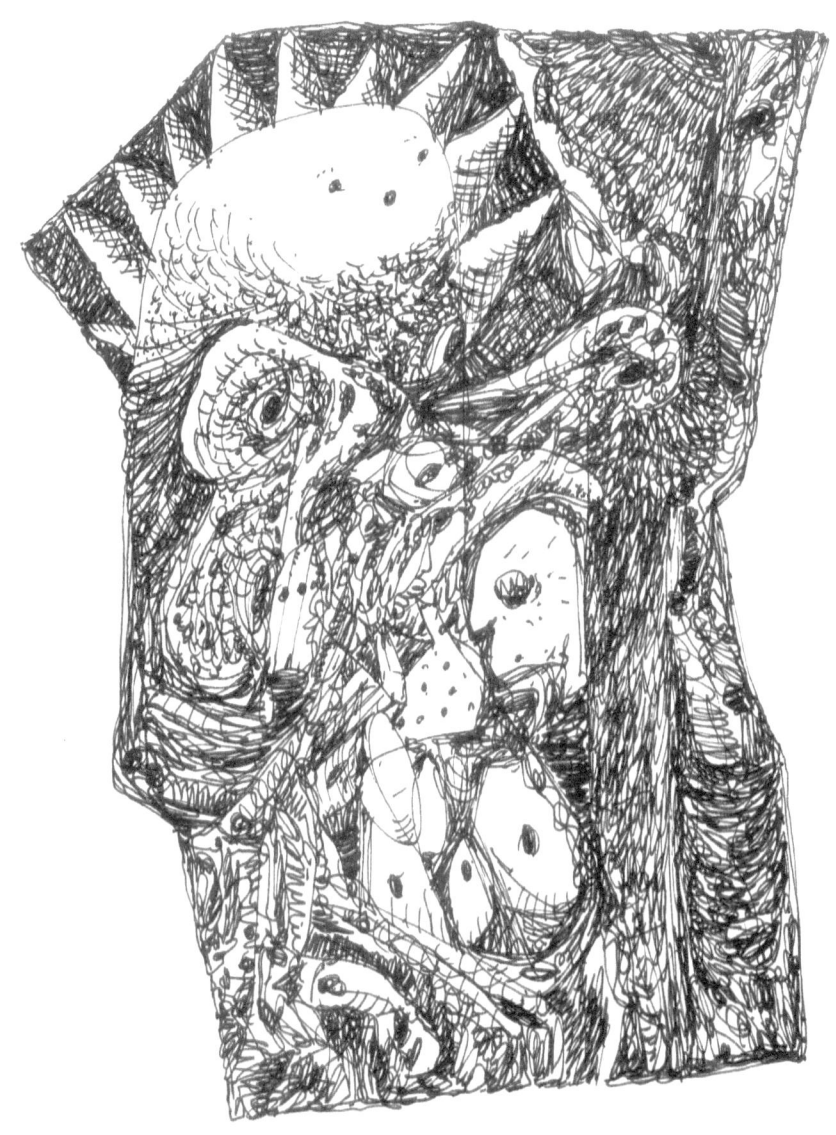

LOS CICLOS

Estuve charlando con tu verdugo.
Un hombre pulcro, amable.
Me dijo que, por ser yo,
podía elegir la forma en que te irías.
Los esquimales, explicó, cuando llegan a viejos
se pierden por los caminos
para que se los coma el oso.
Otros prefieren terapia intensiva,
médicos corriendo alrededor, caños, oxígeno
e incluso un cura a los pies de la cama
haciendo señas como una azafata.

"¿Es inevitable?", le pregunté.
"No hubiera venido hasta acá con esta lluvia", me replicó.
Después habló del ciclo de los hombres, los aniversarios,
la dialéctica estéril del fútbol, la infancia
y sus galpones inmensos con olor a neumáticos.
"Pero", dijo sonriendo,
"las ambulancias terminan devorándose todo".
Así que firmé los papeles
y le pregunté cuándo iba a suceder...
                    ¡Ahora! dijo.
                    Ahora
tengo en mis brazos tu envase retornable.
Y trato de no llorar,
de no hacer ruido,
para que desde lo alto
puedas hallar
la mano alzada de tu halconero.

Fabián Casas

VERDUGO

Juan Perón y Billinghurst

Because of the word for green inside the word for executioner, I am inside the past tense, the present's executioner. I am inside the word inside the intersection of my failure to hear correctly. The mistranslation. It is too easy to find the executioner, in the masculine pronoun, in the butcher shop that's closed today like almost every shop is closed today, a Sunday, in the death of the activist Mariano Ferreyra, of whom remains the paint on the stone wall above the train tracks, just a block away from here. It is difficult to see the color of soundlessness. To make an unbegun. Instead, I vow. To return to this corner every year on this day, a Sunday, which is the day before my birthday. Before my unbegun. To paint the places where the shadow colors the wall of this building the color of that shadow. In the places where the shadows overlap, it will be my birthday. In the places where language ends. In the places where language is the shadow I am throwing on this building. Where one language ends and another begins is only a question of soundlessness.

PULCRO

Juan Perón y Sanchez de Bustamante

Like a friend, he says and wipes his hand diagonally across his shirt. What is dirt if not there is no tracelessness – a hand that has no name in me. The weeds growing out from the stone façade opposite the doorway, where I record how the disintegrating sound of it becomes indistinguishable from the artificial dark, where I wait for the dirt to pluck the string of me. A weight inside his cart. He stops to talk to me, as if his hand were guided by another hand entirely. Like my friend, he says, like somebody who is clean. I wait for the dirt to hold my name back, that overripe fruit that swells inside the disintegrating sound of all the names inside of me, to keep my name from spilling out my mouth. Like somebody who is clean, he says, and the time grinds down into a powder that will not leave their faces.

SEÑAS

Perón y Pasteur

My body is multiplied into photographs, blown around the streets like litter, until it germinates again and again and again inside the cleft in concrete. An old woman walks slowly enough to stop inside my question, her opposite of me rocks back and forth inside her. To demonstrate, she waves her hand between her face and mine, a gesture. Is this what for the body, an impossible forest, a hinge in which I beg to be completed by another? Could walking slowly be hello? Through the windows of the shop behind, the half-assembled mannequins seem to stare at me, my words rising and falling. The future touches the perfect past of me, collides into the stranger. This moment, a hinge, as if hunger were the first bone in any body, the uneaten loaves of bread on the street, a gesture, the same container as shredded paper.

AZAFATA

Perón y Pasteur

No, he says, he has not taken many trips by air except for here. Pointing in the direction of Uruguay, as if *there* were somehow still on this side of the river. Some geographers consider the Río de la Plata a gulf or marginal sea. I am thinking of the *vuelos de la muerte*. As if the river were not river. When the bodies made contact with the water, their names began to dissolve, the husks of they who had borne and called and call for them. They sank into the opposite of calling. It is a funnel-shaped indentation, an estuary. The nouns inside them came apart into the past tense of a verb: *los desaparecidos*. At what point is a river no longer composed of water? Salinity fronts, or haloclines, form at the bottom and on the surface. The stranger tells me it's a word that helps the passengers. At first, I think he means something un-alive and yet essential. There is a sign or a billboard, I can't remember – Envios al Interior, where fresh and brackish waters meet. To cross a body I cannot touch. As if the river were not river. To belong to it, as a kite to the hand that steers it. To be so accustomed to my person suspended, the air no longer harbor. The other side of the river. At what altitude does everything assume the shape of flesh? My body grows closer to a fellow passenger the further I am from ground and yet, aside from turbulence, I do not speak to him.

GALPONES

Paraguay y Azcuénaga

It is not instantaneous, the act of abandoning a city. I want to make you believe. Time clicks shut for the cartographer. I find myself in a city that existed not seven months ago, but three months earlier than the day I first arrived. My missingness weighs more than I do. Time clicks and I can no longer pronounce my name. I keep walking. But this is where the city ends or else continues through the heavy doors. I push the hospital open to get to its definition, the number flashing red for which ghost or premonition, the he she me we stored in here. Inside the empty waiting room, I write a postcard to each of my former lovers. I say, "I want to feed you light from inside the slotted windows." I ask them to record themselves while sleeping. I want to play all these recordings at once, to hear them sleeping simultaneously. I place each postcard on an empty chair and walk outside. A young man finally stops for me, his beauty articulating the boundary between his body and the street. I want to feed him light. I want to feed him anything. He says to me, the word is a construction that houses the materials for construction. The he she me we stored in here. Like childhood, I think, a word dismantled by the growth of the furniture inside it.

HALLAR

Rodríguez Peña y Juncal

I walk through the flaking pressure of this city in order to find it. I move at a regular and fairly slow pace. I translate my craving into someone else's history. I have been learning to walk through walls. The countenance is round and swallowing the pavement, *El Banco de la Nación*, and the nights when I have passed here, its windows throwing my impatience back at me. What of desperation is piled inside its vaults? *Yo sé que tengo el corazón mirando*, the fountain declares to no one in particular. The words are engraved in its stone lip, as if our sentences precede us. I lift one foot and set the other down in turn. The copper adopts the color of the fenced-in grass, as if everything we say was carved into us from the beginning, as if one's age can be calculated by the number of bones that are no longer legible. A teenager talks about her new favorite bar, a place where she will wait for her friends to find her. Two shopkeepers stand outside, carrying on a conversation but not looking – the lamps of their faces yet to be lit by what currency, what underground electricity.

ALZADA

Plaza Miserere

The faces of those who lost the election are quickly becoming paper. They begin to peel away from the billboard, revealing the metal underneath, a dull kind of mirror, reflecting only light and not light's perimeter. The wind is strong. I make my way towards the stranger. He tells me it's a word that could mean many things, like a woman who wants to have an affair. What this has to do with climbing is unclear to me. A girl kneels down to feed the pigeons while her mother watches her. When they gather, larger and less delicate than their predecessors, she takes one in her hands and lifts it to her cheek, a dull kind of mirror. She releases it, and I can sense it, her awe at having invented flight, as if it were an arrow directly into me. I take a photograph of the tree above us. It is only when I put my camera down that I notice it. Hung by its neck from one of the branches, deliberately, with the end of a plastic bag twisted into string, a bird. I could say that I close my eyes and press the camera's eye against me. I could say that I hold it there, that heat, until the batteries run out. I could say that I throw it into the air and walk away.

THE CYCLES

I was chatting with your executioner.
A tidy, friendly man.
He told me, because of who I am,
I could choose the way you'd go.
The Eskimos, he explained, when they get to be old
lose themselves on paths
so that bears will eat them.
Others prefer intensive therapy,
doctors running all around, tubes, oxygen
and even a priest at the foot of the bed
making gestures like a flight attendant.

"Is this inevitable?" I asked him.
"I would not have come so far in this rain," he replied.
After that he talked about the cycle of humans, anniversaries,
the sterile dialectic of soccer, childhood
and its immense warehouses that smell like rubber tires.
"But," he said smiling,
"the ambulances will end up devouring everything."
So I signed the papers
and I asked him when it was going to happen...

                                        Right now! he said.
                                        Now

I have in my arms your returnable bottle.
And I will try not to cry,
to not make a sound,
so that from up high
you can locate
your falconer's raised hand.

Fabián Casas

BREATH, BELLOWED, IN AN EAR UNSEEN

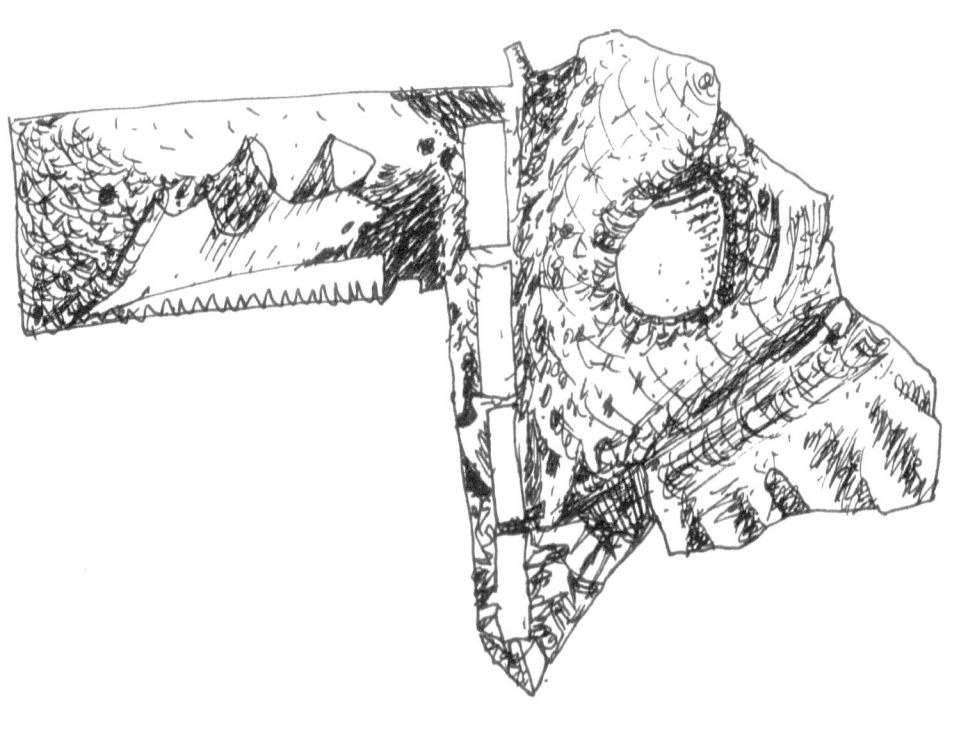

VAPORES

lo que en esa goteja raspadura
de barba humedecida el azulejo, o azul-
ejo de barba amanecida, lo
rociado de esa puntillez, el punto de
    esa toca, en el rocío
de esa puntilla que se raspa, o gota
que lamina: porque la mano que ávida raspa, como una barba el ejo
    azul de esas axilas, o esos muslos – se divisan los muslos en
        la bruma
de humo, en el vapor de esa
corrida: toca rozada, rosa
el lamé, el "por un quítame de allá esas pajas", o manotazo
    de mojado, papas
de loma en la fundidad, o el resbalón
de esas acaloradas mangas, como fleca
    de sudo: o esa transpiración de la que toca, tocada, ese tocado
ese tocado de manuelitas y ese jabón de las vencidas, sofocadas esa
    respiración entrecortada, como de ninfas
venéreas, en el lago de un cuadro, cuadriculan; cuadran, culan
en el kuleo de ese periplo: porque en esas salas, acalambradas
    de lagartos que azules ejos ciñen, o arrastran, babeándose
por los corredores de cortina, *atrapalhada* como una toalla que se
    desliza, o se deja caer, en los tablones
de madera, mad, que toca, madra, toca lo madrastral de ese tocado
    casi gris; pero que en su puntilla, a-
caso deja ver algo? se trasluce esa herida de manteca que el gollo,
    o ese fólego, fuellante, en una oreja que no se ve
o no se sabe de qué cara   es, en ese surco
    que no se ve, esa arruga
        de la transpiración: azoteas de lama,
donde el deseo, en suave irrisión, se hace salpicadura...

Néstor Perlongher

GOTEJA

Viamonte 1770

I begin my translation at the unmarked door outside the sauna. I fold my fingers back to count the months that disappear and return without faces, the sweat behind the stalls. It's a workday – nobody passing seems to know the definition for this yearning, this word trickling from the Portuguese, from a poet's exile. I run my fingers across the hidden, my craving still rising and condensing on the tiles.

AZULEJO

Viamonte y Callao

The reservoir inside continues to evaporate. Even the entrance to the sauna seems to be made out of steam. The old wooden door has been turned into a wall, but the mail slot remains. If I kneel I can see him, my cartographer, rooting through the pile of envelopes. He decides to open two of them. Inside the first, a piece of broken tile. He carries it into the forest of cubicles, looking for the gap it fell away from. Inside the second, the faint song of a bird. Painted feathers fall through a hole in the skylight.

EJO

Viamonte y Rodriguez Peña

The poet hands me not a word but a hinge, a syllable in which only the trace of blue remains. What is a city if not a dictionary of shards? I hold my question mark so I can see it in the window across the street, glass coated with mirror. The roof I can't climb displays its face, sky divided into grid. I lean against the wall. As if plaster had been scraped away to contain her, a woman drawn in pencil. She stands in what seems to be the opening of a cave. She bends her palms at the wrist and faces me. I bend my words to look at her. She casts two shadows, the city and the broken hinge.

ROCIADO, PUNTILLEZ

Luis Dellepiane y Viamonte

The mural tilts a body sideways as if it were floating in someone else's ribcage. He bends his arms at the elbows, covering the part of the wall I think of as his face. At what point does a body dematerialize behind its shame or someone else's architecture? Wildness comes flooding through the cracks in the form of a fern. Wildness at the end of the alley, where two stray dogs begin to screw. A needle punctures the boundary between them, and briefly they're sewn together. When it's all over, one of the dogs just stands there, while the other runs around it in circles. My cartographer walks by on tiptoes, putting the needle back inside its hiding place.

ROCÍO

Viamonte y Luis Dellepiane

Across the mirrored windows, the city doubles and disappears. Someone sweeps up the bits of night between the seams. Exit after exit keeps the bell from sitting still. In the older woman's mouth, my question doubles. She stops for me and sweeps her mind across the seams. In the morning, she begins, and then she begins again: in the morning very early, it's not rain, she says, but something that sounds to me to like moss. What not quite rain is still legible on these streets, what mirror on the window? I am thinking of my love in not this city, of our tendency to only fuck in morning. I crawl through wires to reach him. We double and disappear. I leave my window open. He spreads his sleep against it. He keeps the bell from sitting still. In the morning he begins, and then he begins again: in the morning very early. I translate the night into the not quite rain, the word that he has written there.

PUNTILLA

Viamonte y Montevideo

At this intersection, the streets reverse their names. A tiny leaflet tucks a woman into the seams of the public telephone, multiplies her face into *GIRLS*. I continue in the direction of the river, the reserva ecológica. Before the city put up the fence, it was said to be a good place for cruising. Our body before I even began, inside out inside the reeds. A good place to burn the fence around our name. To fling off the grid and call it wetlands. A little to the east, the horizon keeps rising. I pick up the receiver and hold it out to the passing strangers, waiting for somebody to stop, to prick the lace between us. The sky keeps choking on the river, on the ghost of somebody's child, drowned before I even began.

AXILAS

Viamonte y Paraná

Like bits of folded sky, mesh hangs haphazard from the roof. What was pigeon sways inside its plastic teeth. The wings too vertical, abandoning the body. When I was a boy, I used to watch the others from the sidelines, their arms above their heads. Inside their tufts of animal, I wanted to break my wings. I cut my captors carefully from the catalog and let them dissolve, like bits of sky, on my tongue. What was boy still sways inside them.

BRUMA

Viamonte y Uruguay

I ask someone, a man, his eyes a bit red and wet, walking in the street in a shaky way, just to the left of the curb. He says he doesn't know. The gap between our faces hovers at or near the earth's surface, limiting visibility. Then he says the word out loud, as if that might help, as if a hook might catch a cloud. Across the street, a ghost sputters inside the sign for the old *farmacia*. The woman at the bus stop looks at me and spreads her fingers in the gap. She tells me that *bruma* and *neblina* are synonyms. I am thinking of my brother, tired little vapor walking underwater. When you can't see anything, she says, when there's a lot of humidity, when the airplanes don't take off. The gap between our faces settles into rhyme.

ROZADA

Plaza Lavalle

On the wall behind the swingset, graffiti makes its demand: *Saquen sus rosarios de nuestros ovarios*. I have never held a rosary, but still it hangs around my neck, the violence of religion. As a child, I won a prize for memorizing psalms, hoping to kill the weeds in me. Now I'm a forager, collecting them with ink and paper. A stranger sees me writing and asks me for the time – it's fifteen after two. I show him the word in my hand – he tells me it's a color, but my dictionary just points to color's history, the rupture that precedes it. I ask him if it's somewhere around us, and though I think he lives here in this plaza, he says no – no hay nada rozada.

MANOTAZO

Viamonte y Libertad

Nearing the obelisk, I am shouting to be heard over the noise of jackhammers. The city plunges into itself. The color pushes through in perfect squares. I ask the man in a business suit what it means. He says it's when you put your hand like this up against another person. He pivots his wrist around a memory that was never mine to begin with. I've told this story before. The only time I've ever hit someone, as if he understood something, as if to scrape away the words for what I was. He was my neighbor and I was a boy wearing make-up walking home from rehearsal. I can't remember his name. I swung at him to put a face on me. I broke the bone in one of my hands, the vocabulary that was beginning to grow there. I ask him if it's an act of violence. More or less, he says.

RESBALÓN

Viamonte y Cerrito

At the center of every verb, there's a noun, a stickiness that waits for a person to be walking and then all of a sudden falling down. He bends his knees and tilts his head into the place where I can understand him. The alphabet goes quiet. At the center of every noun, there's a little too much light. I remember when I first started learning parts of speech, the sex club on Halloween, how the other men would look at me as if I were translucent. At the center of every body, there's a bruise. While the stranger offers up his definition, another man walks by. He holds himself up with a cane. As if to demonstrate, his feet point in opposite directions, two arrows that will one day intersect.

MANGAS

Viamonte y 9 de Julio

The pigeons assemble themselves into an almost silver water, a one and vibrating nakedness. I ask the stranger what it means to her. She puts her hand against her sleeve as if to make the body audible. A choreography of trembling. Infinitive: a machine. To rise like a single water, erasing selves in unison. Her words spill into the street. My cartographer waits for her to leave, then soaks them up, just like a sponge. His tongue, a peeled and fading nakedness. A bandage from a wound.

FLECA

Viamonte y 9 de julio

Up against the window of a vacant shop, I press my cheek. I enter through the triangle in glass, where the faded newspaper – the sports section – curls back on itself. The window throws me back as light, an upside-down day it can't absorb. A woman tells me *fleca no existe* but *fleco* is like the thread that hangs down from a scarf. Or an almost arrow, I think. An arrow sharpened momentarily – and then the fallen feathers. Like the model who stares back at me from paper, his beauty peeling back from fringes, from the surface of desire.

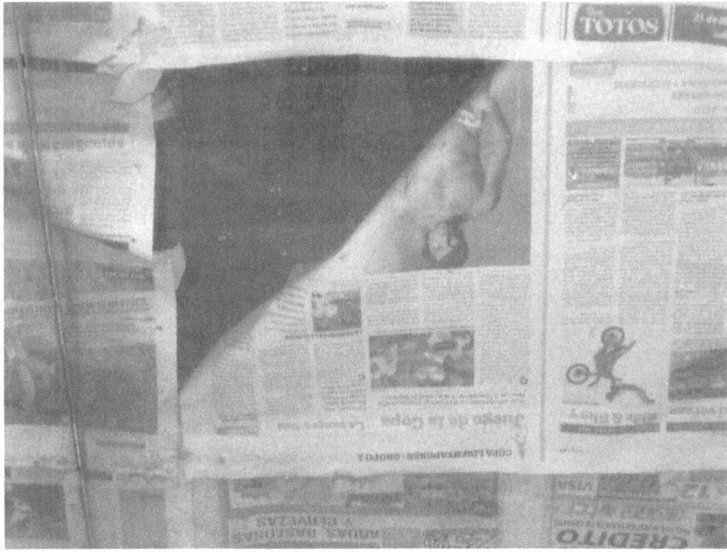

MANUELITAS

Viamonte y Esmeralda

This street engraved by rain and commerce and the exhaust of the exhausted, dogged flesh on flesh. This language of the exiled. A boy hurries past, says he's seen the word before, he can't remember where. This language of the swallowed backwards into sound. Into the tongue that precedes its speaker, the gasping after gut and music. And into this gasping walks my cartographer, pressing his map against the street until it spills: the trap door of meaning.

ENTRECORTADA

Viamonte y Reconquista

Faltering, my translation straying, as on an unmarked street. I lose my footing on an outdated loneliness. Like this monastery, my skin is papered thick with no longer relevance, a palimpsest of former selves. I ask the stranger what it means. He takes my faltering and folds it under his tongue. He pretends to spit it out, but his words keep catching on the clouds inside him. In this city, even weather refuses to be former.

CUADRICULAN, CUADRAN, CULAN

Viamonte y 25 de mayo

An utterance is the sum of otherwise wayward syllables. In the poet's tableau, they float towards the surface of a lake. Remembering themselves as not selves at all, they swim, their bodies a singular fever, writhing, slammed into waking by the words that bubble up from mud. I find myself so far from waking, here, in the banking district, where those who own this country's debt cast their shadows all around. My cartographer takes advantage of the value of his currency. He casts his net, as if he could catch his own shadow, a perfect square of sound detaching from the grid.

KULEO

Viamonte y Alem

Into the open mouth of the city, I climb. I move my body in time with a body I cannot see. The stranger laughs and says it's something erotic, a bit more *argentino*, like when people shake their bottoms in time with music. It's a way of dancing, perhaps, the act of translation, this shaking of words between us.

ALCALAMBRADAS

Viamonte y Alem

Behind the open door, a spark. Someone is giving metal back the memory of fire. I ask him what it means. He says it's like a part of the body that's fallen asleep. When I look into the windows across the street, I see people sending messages through the office walls. Because in this proximity, a choreography. The walls go back to sleep.

ARRASTRAN

Viamonte y Eduardo Madero

Through the corridors of time, somebody's past is skimming the pavement. I'm dragging it behind me, the scar I cannot recognize, the ever-presence of the extinguished. I come upon a poster, rows and rows of faces, a call for justice for the Galician victims of the dictatorships in Spain and South America. *Ayer por nosotros. Hoy por vosotros*, it says. In the grammar of ethics, us rhymes with you. I keep thinking of Emmanuel Levinas, his belief that nonviolence begins in beholding the face of the other. But then I think of the violence of my own country, and the words of Darren Wilson, the police officer who murdered Michael Brown. He told the jury that Brown "had the most intense aggressive face." He said, "it looks like a demon." It: the faceless pronoun. He used this word to unbehold, to blot out the life of an unarmed man.

I follow Perlongher's shadows. In 1976, at the beginning of the dictatorship, he was detained for three months because of his political activities. What demon did his captors believe they saw? What kept them from doing away with him completely?

ATRAPALHADA

Mariquita Thompson y Alicia M de Justo

Some trees send down aerial roots, pouring sky all over their secret insides. The stranger hasn't heard of it – it's not a word in his language, his secret insides, but a piece of living tissue embroidered on another. He politely steps to the side of the poem. It's climbing up the escalator moving down, refusing to not belong. The poem is an official citizen of its own disorder. Eventually, it goes out of print and loses its passport. The authorities bar the entry to the escalator, where someone has put a potted plant on every step, perhaps in memory of the poem, the border that refuses to be border.

DESLIZA

Paseo Patonal de Puerto Madero

River, like a body that convulses, or lets itself shrink, hemmed by harbor. I'm climbing backwards up the arc of gravity. The stranger tells me it's a kind of falling, smooth and with direction, curved. Like the newspaper that floats, or lets itself disintegrate, in water. Like the Puente de la Mujer, the sky poured into its single mast. The history of human falling. When it swings, the ground breaks in half, purposefully, making way for water. Each person is a story that floats, waiting to disintegrate.

MADRASTRAL

Paseo Patonal de Puerto Madero

When the people walk towards me is a way of saying past me: across this footbridge, over the muddy canal. Their shadows touch the shadows of this touched one. As if they themselves descend the rails, relinquish flesh for flickering water. Down the rungs of light into: the across, the towards, the over, the down, the between. The buoyant preposition. The hovering song of planks between self and other. Across this footbridge, the poem and the writer trading places. Colder than a kiss of *madrastra* is what Alejandro tells me: your mother dies and your father marries another woman. My cartographer wed his shadow. He dressed her up and gathered all the roses that they threw at her. He said they were only trading places, but when the audience went home, he turned off the lights and left her. Alone on the stage: the hovering song between a shadow and a mother.

TRASLUCE

Paseo Patonal

My cartographer climbs his invisible staircase until the motion of climbing starts to carry him. Like light, the verb passes through its subject. The stain of the body giving way, giving back its way. Unbecoming in mid-air. Way gives weight, in order for air to know its lungs, the fact of it, a breathing. I ask the stranger if he can tell me what it means. The stain of always looking keeps me looking. I take a photograph of the river's height: 23 meters. This desire for measure. A number is never but the stain of rising, falling. He says it's to make oneself transparent. As if this were beauty. The stain of desire. As if happening could be if he could see through me.

GOLLO

Paseo Patonal de Puerto Madero

I've always had trouble with gravity, unable to pull myself away. I've always had trouble with I've, such invasive coiling. The pronoun swallows half a verb, sends in its soldiers to clean things up, and then reaches out with a lukewarm apostrophe. Meanwhile, the city pulls the continent past itself, tugging on its skin. In their fine clothes, the strangers pass me with such determination – I'm afraid to interrupt them. He doesn't have the time, the young man tells me. As if time were a growth he had removed. A window slammed at the end of every working day. Meanwhile, the poem is on all fours, licking up the words that fall, half-eaten, from his mouth.

FÓLEGO, FUELLANTE

Olga Cossettini y Mariquita Thompson

The air inside Perlongher passed through the bellows of another language. His echoes ride the ocean currents into the dirty river lapping on this shore. Here, in Puerto Madero, in the shadows of the high-rises, I lean against the non-descript and orderly. My friends say this neighborhood doesn't even feel like their country. Perhaps that's what Kissinger was thinking of when he secretly told the generals, "If there are things that have to be done, you should do them quickly." One translation of *Fuella*: the third person singular of fucking, fucking up, or fucking over. The difference that a preposition makes. Sometimes a hinge becomes a hook. I lean into the fact of my complicity. The stranger says he doesn't know exactly, but maybe it's like this, like what a plant does, his hands cupped and softly opening, unfolding. The poem keeps returning the heavy breath it gathers, thrusting, shaking off its own gesture after gesture bending down: this unextinguished blossoming.

ARRUGA

Parque Costanera Sur

I was sculpted from the every ever touched me. Forty years revolving, a barge tossing moan across water. I follow the sound. This park, a liminal place. The pavement evaporates into public craving, a barely visible pool in which a previous is floating, gasping. The old man answers my question by laughing, pointing to the marks on his skin. *You see?* I can almost read them, written on his flesh, the errant codes. Their microscopic mouths, opening and closing. As if translation too were cruising, wanting the nakedness of the error, kneeling down and taking it, literally.

AZOTEAS

Camino Lagarto

Out here the land becomes a laminated : star : a resting point for all that's wild and migrating. You feel the hot breath of the airplane taking off and mind takes to gathering feathers. Little contrails clouding up the surface. You put them in your cap and think of your friend and his red *capucha*. And you want to say there is no cap on sky but here you are again in your language, your primary here, and it's hard to hear again, it's hard to stay in touch. Head and headphones under hood and the exhalations : rising.

STEAM

what in that trickling scrape
of moistened beard the tile, or blue-
glaze of dawning beard,
sprayed from that needlework, the tip of
        that bonnet, in the dew
of that lace that is scraped, or droplet
that glosses: because the hand that eagerly scrapes, like a beard, the glaze
        blue of those armpits, or those thighs – can make out thighs in
            the fog
of smoke, in the steam of that
eruption: bonnet rubbed, rosy
the lamé, the "over nothing at all," or slap
            of wetness, wild
pickings in the dissipation, or the slip
of those fevered sleeves, like fringe
        from sweat: or that perspiration that handles, handled, that headdress,
that headdress of handlings and that lather of the vanquished, suffocated that
        gasping breath, like venereal
nymphs, in the lake of a tableau, they amass; they tabulate, they ass
in the assing of that odyssey: because in those rooms, cramped
        by lizards that blue glazes gird, or drag, salivating
through the corridors of a curtain, *tangled* like a towel that
        slides, or is dropped, on the planks
of wood, mud, that handles, mutter, handles what is stepmotherly in that headdress
        nearly gray: but in its needlework, per-
haps reveals something? that creamy bruise that shines through the hole
        or that breath, bellowed, in an ear unseen
or unknown from what face   it is, in that unseen
    groove, that wrinkle
        of perspiration: rooftops of ooze,
where desire, in soft ridicule, becomes splashing...

Néstor Perlongher

WHERE OUR ERROR REPOSES

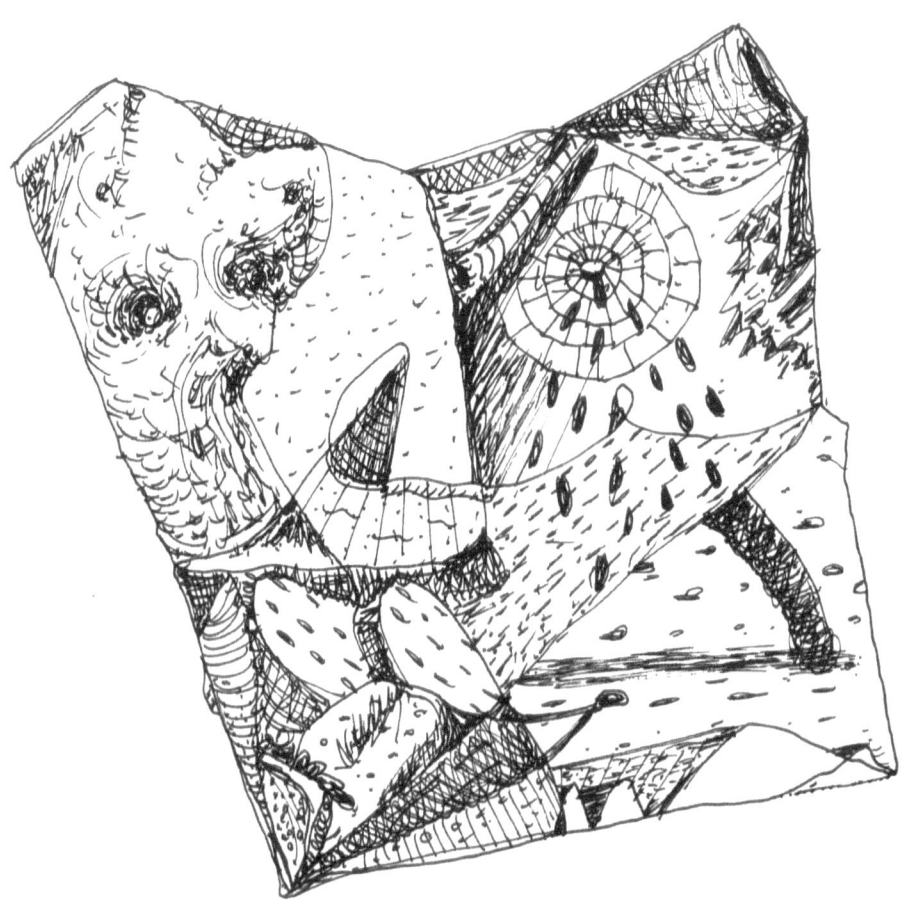

LO QUE SE LLEVA EL VIENTO EN SU RUMOR

Adentro, o afuera
la mirada empobrece
o regenera. Arte
menor, lo que se lleva
el viento en su rumor
Lo que va transformando
su ser y deja, huellas
para así repetirse
en variación. Semilla
al fin, nada afuera
del marco del paisaje
ofrece yo quisiera
para mí, para ti
mi voz de arte menor

Entonces, quizás sí
podría decir no
a todo monumento
para dejarnos ir
después de urdir esteras
con las frágiles fibras
del corazón. Esteras
donde otros soñarán
el incesante sueño
de ser para dejar
de ser tan dulcemente
que acune el dormir
de aquellos que vendrán

Lo que vendrá. ¿A que?
A mejorar el mundo
en arte menor, parte
intentando borrar

aquel dolor que sufre
y otorga. Historia
donde reposa nuestro
error. ¿Cuál? No saber
somos sólo en aquello
que dejamos ir. Cara
inversa de incierta
plusvalía, mirada
de niña que nos sigue,
un menos de dolor
Orfebrería donde
hoy, quisiera dejarte,
voz de arte, menor

Diana Bellessi

HUELLAS

Mario Bravo y Avenida Díaz Velez

My cartographer skins his knee on the mortality of strangers. He collapses the city between one word and another into the museum of broken sirens. I arrive at the seventh block, where a vine curls around and around this tree, threatening to choke it, like a name. I hold my breath. My cartographer is eating language. My cartographer skins his knee. Etymologically, a parasite is a person eating at someone else's table, but we have seen that writing and wood become inseparable. Etymologically, I hold my breath. The name I cannot swallow is spreading, like a vine, into the absence of a window, crowding out the etymology with its unrelenting green. I collapse, I arrive, I cannot swallow, I do not possess. I ask a teenage boy what it means. He makes of his body a pivot. He bends to the ground to put his hand in imaginary concrete. He puts his hand in my hand, and I lower my cartographer into that goodbye, into that wet hollow where he continues walking upside down.

URDIR

Venezuela y Quintino Bocayura

My failure becomes a dictionary. In retrospect, I want to offer an eraser to every stranger. I ask them to run it over me until the bricks have fallen away. A tall man with long hair, in his left hand a cigarette, approaches me. He is so kind to me. It means to make a plan in secrecy, he tells me, and then he tries to bury that airlessness by pushing down his hands. Across the street, there are broken bottles stuck into cement to keep intruders out. I cut my fingers on my dictionary. I am an eraser, burning. Inside the locked and rusted newsstand, the only light in winter is erasing the city and copying it over again from memory. When I get home, the tall man will send me an email, telling me the word – he's been holding it up to the light of his computer – more closely resembles weaving. I cut his message into long strips of fire, the only light in winter, and begin to interlace them.

ESTERAS

Venezuela y Fortunato Devoto

If I look up, a power line traces these migrations. This noun is larger than a window but it fits inside the glass. It helps them to touch each other, this side of the street and its double. Touching peels the tree down into adjective, into window, and so I mistake this – the word for this – for the breath of that on me. The old man cups his ear, and when he opens his mouth, the T becomes a P – it means you have to wait. *Hay que esperar.* There is having to wait. There is no indicated pronoun, there is only the having to wait. If I were to translate his translation, if I were to take one hundred photographs, I would choose the moments where his mouth were closed, tape them together, and feed them into the projector. I wait until my errors start breathing. There is only the slow procession of light, rectangle after rectangle rising.

The girl wants to provide the perfect definition. I try to reassure her. There is crawling across the mind. She says *to put a blanket down. In the soul.* She says *to take the time to reflect on something.* She says *that's what it means to me.* I don't want to use quotation marks. I want to put down the mistake, like a blanket, in the soul. My blanket starts breathing. Why is the proof of winter an artifact of previous weather? From this side of the street, there is a leaf curled in on itself. There is no indicated pronoun. There is blotting out the opposite wall in the shape of a leaf curled in on itself. Why is the proof of winter. There is no discernible ending. If I were to remove it, could I see through the other side of the street to the sky behind it?

ACUNE

Rosario y Avenida La Plata

I cannot bring him with me, to this city, my him, all verticality dissolves when my open mouth, looking up at him, my love, which is the name for this month when I am gone. I sleep beside a pile of books equal to the weight of him, chosen for me by him. I walk the city with my paper colander, my cartographer. The pen is a deficient eye. My open mouth, dissolving. When I develop this photograph, I will see what I do not see originally. Looking dissolves. The same is true of poetry. The I is a deficient eye, a colander. Waiting for the bus, a boy becomes a woman. To be waiting is a palimpsest. She is mouth-reading the newspaper in her hands and his lips are moving, involuntarily, a language equal to the weight of him. She holds her left elbow with her right hand and she swings her arms back and forth in the air. For me, a child equal to the weight of me. He makes his way to his seat. Dissolving into the city, the open mouth between us.

OTORGA

Otamundi y Bogotá

The bookseller tells me there's a saying, *Él que calla, otorga.* Along Calle Bogotá, the recently felled branches are piled around the trunks of their trees. One who remains silent makes an offering. The yellow caution tape, a slack perimeter: *Haciendo Buenos Aires.* The city wraps each injury around itself until it grows into a limb. One who makes an offering. My cartographer begins to remove the books from their encasements. He folds the edges back in place, as if the language were still inside, and returns the cellophane husks to the shelves. *Lo que no dice con las palabras, lo dice con ese silencio.* Two women are sweeping what is not said with words, the sawdust, into the street. My cartographer hangs the books from ghost branches with yellow caution. I graft my silence to my translation, where slack perimeter becomes a limb.

PLUSVALÍA

Parque el Centenario

I begin my translation before I know what I am looking for. I am walking away from the little digital pool in which my solitude can't get wet. I am walking with my new friend, between the windows we can't see through and the fucking. The first word he teaches me is the opposite of winter. He leads me here. The opposite of solitude cuts all the pockets off my clothes and tosses them into the lake. Ten months pass and he is gone and I fall into the concentrated light.

I have never seen it like this, the park with arrows of dusk moving across it. The neighborhood lifts off the ground a little. I ask a stranger what it means. To him it is a Marxist concept, the difference between what a person earns and their labor. The space between the solitudes get smaller. They start referring to themselves as us. The night with arrows of not me moving, before time teaches me to be anything. A colder city is memory. I know I should be going now, my hands are getting numb. The drinking fountain is broken, but there's a piece of bread inside it. I recognize my mouth on the part that's chewed away. I'm thirsty. It must be my translation.

ORFEBRERÍA

Luis Maria Drago y Lavalleja

The sun goes off like a faucet and the city, suspended from its wire, spills into the intersection. I hold my open palms in front of me, the echo I cannot otherwise. When the blank pages touch inside my dictionary, the city begins to curve. I think about sex, an equals sign between the body and its zero. The words start crawling out from their hollows. A young man tells me it makes a sound in him, a question mark that recognizes him, but he doesn't know how to describe it. He is the echo I cannot touch, a precious metal. I am the blank page leaking. The light lodges itself, like gold, in the folds of plastic, the vertical assemblage of oranges erasing gravity.

My cartographer erases graffiti. I set my alarm and return, just before dawn, to paint the wall as best as I can from memory. When I finish, I wait for the stranger who tells me it's a very old word, one part heat and one part hollow. He wants to know where I come from – he has a cousin who lives on Staten Island. Between the echo and where I come from, he makes a gesture, an equals sign between the worker and the act of shaping fire. It hangs in the air, a precious metal, long after he returns his hands to his side.

WHAT THE WIND CARRIES IN ITS RUMOR

Inside, or outside
the gaze impoverishes
or revives. Minor
art, what the wind
carries in its rumor
What goes on transforming
its essence and leaves, imprints
to be repeated
in variation. Seed
at last, nothing outside
the frame the landscape
offers I would like
for me, for you
my voice of minor art

So, perhaps yes
I could say no
to every monument
to let us go
after weaving mats
with the fragile fibers
of the heart. Mats
upon which others will dream
the incessant dream
of being in order to let go
of being so sweetly
that it cradles the sleep
of those who will come of

What's to come. What for?
To better the world
in minor art, in part
trying to erase

that pain it suffers
and bestows. History
where our error
reposes. Which one? Not knowing
we only exist in that
which we let go. Reverse
face of uncertain
gain, gaze
of the girl that follows us,
a lessening of pain
Goldsmithing where
today, I would like to leave you,
voice of art, minor

Diana Bellessi

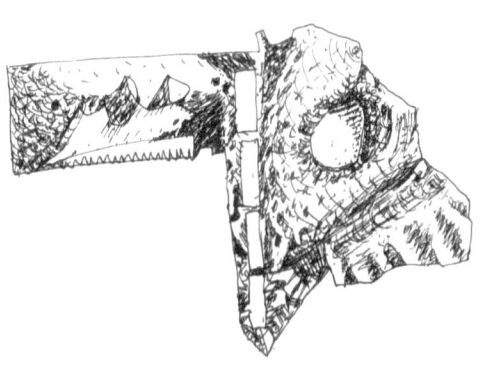

FUTURE SOMATICS TO DO LIST
a love letter to *street gloss*: to brent

by jen hofer

is there a method for moving when the mode of locomotion is no longer sure?

no longer speakable?

ya no movimiento llano, memento mori, momento motor. ¿torpeza al sur de la destreza, bienvenida tropieza y bienaventurada al andar?

no longer transparent?

"language is situational," rajiv mohabir says. the air fills with brittle words? the light is tender. which questions can be unasked?

it was never speakable.

in attempting to walk alongside, neighborliness occurs. a concourse? a recurrence? a rent?

how quiet do we need to be to hear the diagnosis? the deficit?

erasure is a practice. countering erasure is a practice. the gap between gaping. being questionable is being answerable?

where is gloss glass? when is it glaze? civics ? the gaze beyond the engraved?

the body is gloss? chartreuse shoots blanketing over a shape? anthills?

what can we actually unlearn?

what does it cost to be on that corner? what water was their grave?

the finding of language previously unlost is an architecture of slowing in place, staying to say.

in the sway of unquiet grasses soon to disappear, lupine, poppy, coreopsis, brittle bush, alien spores.

"you go to the land and ask what technology to use," monica mody says. decolonizing decisiveness. is all birth after-life?

speech through the generations becomes speechlessness. foreign object under the tongue. hinging jaw or knee or mirror.

naming is disembodying or offering body? describing a circuit or spiral. systemic or asking again and again cada vez más to unbuild.

cataclysm? catastrophe? catalytic?

the translator is translated. shedding? shreds? shards?

el gato o el gatillo, lo apuntado o lo que apunta. ¿lo que fluye? denota. plume or loom as a mountain or purposeful pause? lo que detona.

is all after-life birth? birds? bloom?

beginning in one place and moving to another. trans. position. potion. collusion. kissing cousin.

NOTES

The quote from Constanza Svidler in the preface comes from her unpublished essay, "Walking the City, Mapping History: Of Plaques, Memorials, and Cenotaphs in Buenos Aires."

"Ciudades- tres," by Alejandro Méndez, was originally published in *Chicos Índigo* (Bajo la luna, 2007).

"Situación para romper un hechizo," by Mercedes Roffé, was originally published in *La Ópera Fantasma* (Bajo la luna, 2005). This poem has also been translated by Judith Filc and appears in the journal *Talisman* and the book *Ghost Opera* (co-im-press, 2017).

"Los ciclos," by Fabián Casas, was originally published in *El spleen de Boedo* (Vox, 2005) and appears in his collected works, *Horla City y otros* (Emecé, 2010).

"Vapores," by Néstor Perlongher, was originally published in *Alambres* (Último Reino, 1987) and appears in his collected works, *Poemas completos* (La Flauta Mágica, 2014). Roberto Echavarren, Jen Hofer, and Constanza Svidler provided instrumental feedback for the translation of this poem.

"Lo que se lleva el viento en su rumor," by Diana Bellessi, was originally published in *Sur* (Libros de Tierra Firme, 1998) and appears in her collected works, *Tener lo que se tiene* (Adriana Hidalgo Editora, 2009).

The photograph that accompanies "Azafata" is from *Carteles de la memoria*, an installation by Grupo de Arte Callejero at Parque de la Memoria in Buenos Aires.

DREAM, CHEW, LEAK, STUMBLE, SPIRAL, LISTEN, TRACE, TOUCH, RETURN.

A CONVERSATION WITH BRENT ARMENDINGER

Greetings! Thank you for talking to us about your process today! Can you introduce yourself, in a way that you would choose?

I'm Brent. I use he/him/his pronouns. I'll try to use this space to tell you some things that aren't in my bio. My first name is my father's middle name, and I grew up in the house where he was raised by his grandparents in Warsaw, a very small town in Western NY. My dad worked in a factory that made parts for Ford, and my mom was a legal secretary - now they're both retired. I was the first person in my family to graduate from college. I've lived in Annandale-on-Hudson (Bard), San Francisco, and Ann Arbor, and now I live in Los Angeles with my husband, Joe Gallucci, who is a media archivist and crossword aficionado. We got married in May of this year and our processional was "The Rainbow Connection" by Kermit the Frog. We both hate capitalism and sometimes fantasize about opening a queer bar called Comrades and Curmudgeons. What else? I love deciduous trees, succulents, oxygen, handwriting, palimpsests, twilight, etymologies, ice cream, swimming, and of course, poetry.

Why are you a poet/writer/artist/translator?

Writing a poem, for me, is a way to practice being attentive to my surroundings, as well as a way to open myself to impermanence and not-knowing. I've likened it to walking across quicksand. As soon as I think I know where the ground is, it changes. So it has to be more about moving than standing, and it's not so much my legs that are moving but the ground itself, the quicksand.

Certainty is momentary and there are these instances of sinking, sliding, falling, floating, in which I find myself writing towards the strangeness that is simultaneous to facts. As Anne Carson writes, "what we are engaged in when we do poetry is error,/the willful creation of error,/the deliberate break and complication of mistakes/out of which may arise/unexpectedness."[1]

---

1 Anne Carson, "Essay on What I Think About Most," *Men in the Off Hours* (Knopf, 2000).

As a translator, I'm an amateur, and this book arose out of following my errors, my not-knowing, into the streets.

When did you decide you were a poet/writer/artist (and/or: do you feel comfortable calling yourself a poet/writer/artist, what other titles or affiliations do you prefer/feel are more accurate)?

I don't know that I can pinpoint an exact moment, and the truth is I prefer to say that I make poems. There are, however, specific people who helped me experience the magic and possibility of poetry when I was young, such as my fifth grade teacher, Bill Heller, my first poetry teacher, Robert Kelly, and Adrienne Rich in her book *What Is Found There*. I'm grateful to each of them for showing me that I could be with, in, and alongside poetry.

What's a "poet" (or "writer" or "artist") anyway? What do you see as your cultural and social role (in the literary / artistic / creative community and beyond)? How does this interface with what you do as a translator and/or in your pedagogy?

I think that poetry can model an ethics of encountering what we don't immediately understand, both about ourselves and the world around us. I talk about this a lot with my students, because young people are still being taught that there's something wrong (either with them or the poem itself) if they don't "get" a poem on the first reading. I like to remind them that a poem is first and foremost an experience, that the world is full of things we don't understand, and that it's good to practice not turning away from those things. As a poet, I think my first responsibility is to give agency to language itself. As Robert Kelly writes, "[n]ot to use the words to sell yourself or your ideas."[2] This is, of course, the task of a lifetime.

I also think it's my responsibility to write from and alongside our times, from the minutiae of everyday existence to some of our most pressing struggles, not from a place of comfortable distance, but of intimate contact. This means, as Brenda Hillman has written, leaving the writing desk "to engage with others in public spaces. It is then the potential of each word comes forward."[3] It means showing up for striking teachers and for my neighbors who are being displaced. It means engaging not only with human neighbors

---

2 Robert Kelly, "Writing Is," *Red Actions* (Black Sparrow Press, 1995).

3 Brenda Hillman, "Reportorial Poetry, Trance & Activism," *Practical Water* (Wesleyan University Press, 2009).

but with plant and animal and mineral neighbors. As a teacher, it means making more space for poetry to be in the world. My students teach me things all the time. They are capable of doing things with language that I simply can't, and finding ways to nurture that is one of the best things about my job. As a teacher I face the same questions that I do as a poet -- what does it mean to honestly communicate, to ethically respond to the facts of another life?

In this book, as a translator, it means giving my attention to writing that is very different than my own. It means really engaging, with my body, with the public life of language, with the city of Buenos Aires and the people who live there.

Talk about the process or instinct to move this project into book form. How and why did this happen? Have you had this intention for a while? What encouraged and/or confounded this (or a book, in general) coming together? Was it a struggle? How did this unique hybrid of translation and personal practice evolve?

Originally, I traveled to Buenos Aires because I was interested in learning about and working with Eloisa Cartonera - a collective of writers, designers and activists who make very simple, inexpensive, beautiful books out of cardboard that they buy from cartoneros, people who collect it on the street to make a living. Founded in 2001, originally as a response to the economic crisis, their work has spawned a revolution in cartonera publishing throughout Latin America and beyond. While I was volunteering with the folks at Eloisa Cartonera, I also decided to do a writing project. I envisioned this as a way to connect more with the city, and I knew that I wanted to incorporate translation somehow. I've always been interested in site-specific work, ritual, and unconventional ways of understanding geography, but this was a definite turning point in bringing these kinds of procedures into my own poetic practice.

I loved being led to (and by) poets whose work was new to me as the project unfolded, and I loved meeting the poets themselves and discussing their work with them. I was drawn to Alejandro Méndez's haunting queer lyrics, to Mercedes Roffé's use of surreal and poignant instructions, to the immediacy in Fabián Casas' conversational, edgy poems, to Néstor Perlongher's irreverent and erotic wordplay, and to Diana Bellessi's philosophical meditations. I loved that while translating their poems, I was made to do something with my body and that I couldn't predict where they would take me. It felt important that I give up some of my own autonomy as a North American engaged in the complicated act of translation. I also became very interested in the idea that words are physical and that language is actually embedded in the street. I'm thinking here of the artist Joseph Grigely, who writes, "Imagine if every word we spoke became palpable and dropped from our lips as we spoke."[4]

So how did all of this turn into a book? What you are currently looking at has gone through many, many iterations over the last several years. I've been lucky enough to be able to take three separate trips to Buenos Aires in order to work on it. As the book began to take shape, I had to think a lot about form, about how to create a visual manifestation of my process for the reader, while maintaining the integrity of the poets' work. Yes, I was doing this very experimental thing, but I also wanted the translations themselves to be as faithful as possible to the original poems, and that of course is not easy, especially with someone like Perlongher, who delights in double- and triple-entendre and incorporates dialect and other languages into his poems. But there's something amazing about stepping into a syntax that's so wildly different than my own, feeling it push against the limits of my voice.

As the book evolved, it became more and more a way for me to think about translation and language itself, about the ways it lives inside the body and moves between bodies, about cities and the slippage between private and public experience. This book only contains about ¼ of the raw material I generated while working on the project -- I have several notebooks filled with my notes from other walks and translations. It wasn't easy for me to let go of all of this, but at a certain point I began to feel myself forcing the work beyond its organic stopping place. I also wanted the book to have some spaciousness, to not just be a crowded compendium of everything I did. I don't think a book can or even should be perfect, but I'm really happy with where this one landed.

Did you envision this collection as a collection or understand your process as writing or making specifically around a theme while the work itself was being made? How or how not?

I didn't really conceive of it as a book in the beginning, but as I continued to work on these walking translations, it became clearer and clearer that something was coalescing.

---

4   Joseph Grigely: St. Cecilia (Frances Young Tang Teaching Museum, 2007).

What formal structures or other constrictive practices (if any) do you use in the creation of your work, beyond this project? Have certain teachers or instructive environments, or readings/writings/work of other creative people informed the way you work/write?

I've been incorporating a lot more ritual practice into my writing, and I have been particularly inspired by CAConrad's brilliant (Soma)tic exercises. I love the experience of consciously living with the raw materials of a poem before even beginning to write. A couple of years ago, I did a series of walking meditations in the Arroyo Seco, a paved channel that flows near my apartment in Los Angeles. I dressed in all red and carried a red umbrella, meditated on the drought and the people who were living on the banks of the Arroyo and had been pushed out by the city. I generated lots of language, and then I shaped this into a little collection of mesostics, a form invented by John Cage.

Last fall, I had a residency at Blue Mountain Center in the Adirondacks, and I decided to visit the same 13 trees over a number of days, generate a couple of lines for each, and then collage these into poems. I loved the durational aspect of this, the experience of continual returning, of opening up to something I hadn't noticed about each of these trees before.

I work a lot with collage. In my first book, *The Ghost in Us Was Multiplying*, I made a number of poems by combining writing from looking out windows and responding to photographs in the newspaper. I also do a lot of re-ordering and writing between the lines, and I really like writing poems backwards, word by word, which is a technique Carmen Giménez Smith introduced to me and my students when she came to visit my class a while ago. I also love syllabics, especially as a generative tool -- I find it's a great way to push me beyond my ingrained cadences.

I am fortunate to have been nourished by the work of so many different creative people. Among my teachers, those who were particularly instrumental to my growth as a poet include Robert Kelly at Bard, Carmen Giménez Smith and her San Francisco workshop, Thylias Moss and Anne Carson at Michigan, and Brenda Hillman at the Napa Valley Writers Conference and the Community of Writers. There are far too many writers whose work is important to me for me to name, but in Los Angeles, I feel a special kinship to the work of Sesshu Foster, Amina Cain, and Jen Hofer, whose practice as a translator and language justice activist is deeply inspiring. I'm also super lucky to have wonderful poet-friends like Rae Gouirand and Jessica Rae Bergamino who help me keep returning to the page. What else? I find that visual art really helps me reconceptualize the way I approach writing. A few artists whose work is essential to me are Agnes Martin, Yoko Ono, David Wojnarowicz, Theresa Hak-Kyung Cha, Cecilia Vicuña, and Felix Gonzalez-Torres. Finally, I am so inspired by my neighbors and comrades in the Los Angeles Tenants Union, by the creativity it takes to survive and fight back against displacement.

Speaking of monikers, what does your title represent? How was it generated? Talk about the way you titled the book, and how your process of naming (individual pieces, sections, etc) influences you and/or colors your work specifically.

The title is partly a play on words, as it takes "gloss" from glossary. I'm also thinking about gloss as a sheen, a filmy, ephemeral substance that adheres to a surface, the way in which a word might adhere to a street. The section titles are all taken from my translations of the original poems into English. I chose them fairly intuitively. The individual prose poems are all titled with the words they're attempting to define.

What does this particular work represent to you as indicative of your method/ creative practice? your history? your mission/intentions/hopes/plans?

As I mentioned elsewhere, this book represents a fairly significant shift in my practice given its coming to be through a conscious use of ritual and procedural poetics. I think it's certainly still connected to my previous work in terms of the intuitive approach to language, the syntax experiments, the queer content, and the overall emphasis on the body. As a poet, I've never sunk into sentences before in the way I have with this book, so that has been exciting. I've also never incorporated translation into my practice to such an extent, and I'm interested in the possibility of deepening that by working on a single book by one author. Ultimately, this book represents my intentions to take risks as a writer, to follow language in unexpected directions, to give attention to the work of other writers, to bring the body into poetry (and vice versa), to expand and deepen my perceptions.

What does this book DO (as much as what it says or contains)?

Dream, chew, leak, stumble, spiral, listen, trace, touch, return.

What would be the best possible outcome for this book? What might it do in the world, and how will its presence as an object facilitate your creative role in your community and beyond? What are your hopes for this book, and for your practice?

I hope that people will read it, of course, even/especially people who don't consider themselves to be poets. I hope they'll think about the layers and layers of experience that exist in every physical location, including the intersections they pass through every day. I want poems to replace Google Maps! At the very least, I hope people are inspired to move around without a map telling them what to do (map here could be replaced by many emblems of authority). I hope they're inspired to interact a little more with strangers. I hope that readers are led to more work by the different authors I've translated and to Argentinian poetry in general. I hope the book can contribute to conversations about translation and experimental approaches to the craft, about ritual and procedural poetics.

Let's talk a little bit about the role of poetics and creative community in social and political activism, so present in our daily lives as we face the often sobering, sometimes dangerous realities of the Capitalocene. How does your process, practice, or work otherwise interface with these conditions?

These conditions enter my poems because they're moving in and through every one of us. When I write about/from/alongside them, I'm trying to create a space of contact, as much for myself as for my readers. I'm trying to really *be* here, in the midst of all of it. Several of the poems in my first book attempt to confront the abuses of the US military, especially in Iraq and Afghanistan. I went to a lot of demonstrations in the time when I was writing that book, and I've honestly been shocked at how the anti-war movement has all but disappeared in this country in recent years. Props to Code Pink for keeping up the pressure! There's also a long poem in my first book that responds to the Deepwater Horizon oil spill, and there are poems about my experience being queer and HIV+. In this book, it felt necessary to confront the legacy of the dictatorship in Argentina, including how the United States enabled it, as well as the role of hedge-fund investors in strangling the economy. There are also poems that reference police brutality and drone strikes, because the realities of my country don't leave me when I leave its borders. A lot of the poems I'm writing now are haunted by the climate crisis. Of course, it's not enough to just write about these realities, to point at them from a distance. And besides, pointing doesn't make for good poetry - we have to let the experience live inside us. We have to show up in the ways that we can - maybe that's by taking to the streets, maybe it's in the often less glamorous work of organizing, maybe it's something else entirely. Writing and reading are ways to practice "being with," and while insufficient on their own, I find them to be indispensable.

I'd be curious to hear some of your thoughts on the challenges we face in speaking and publishing across lines of race, age, ability, class, privilege, social/cultural background, gender, sexuality (and other identifiers) within the community as well as creating and maintaining safe spaces, vs. the dangers of remaining and producing in isolated "silos" and/or disciplinary and/or institutional bounds?

Community is real, ongoing work, and it has to include as many different voices as possible, especially those who have been marginalized. I also think spaces for particular communities are crucial for individual and cultural survival, and it seems to me these spaces actually expand what's possible in our larger communities. Of course, there's a difference between a community and an institution, and for me, it all comes down to power and access. On that note, I'm particularly inspired by the radical work The Operating System is doing to change the culture of publishing and break down barriers. I couldn't be happier that this book has found a home here.

ABOUT THE POETS

Alejandro Méndez was born in Buenos Aires in 1965. He has published six books of poetry: *Variaciones Goldberg* (Ediciones del Dock, 2003); *Medley* (Suscripción, Larga distancia, 2003); *Tsunami* (Crunch! Editores, 2005); *Chicos índigo* (Bajo la luna, 2007); *Cosmorama* (Ediciones Liliputienses, 2013), and *Pólder* (Bajo la luna, 2014). In 1993, he translated Francis Ponge's *L'Asparagus* into Spanish. Méndez coordinates *Las Elecciones Afectivas*, the first self-managed curatorship of contemporary Argentinian poetry: laseleccionesafectivas.blogspot.com.ar. He is also the editor of the online poetry journal *Deshielo*: deshieloediciones.wordpress.com. Méndez currently teaches in the creative writing program at the Universidad de las Artes in Buenos Aires. His personal website is chicosindigo.blogspot.com.ar.

Mercedes Roffé was born in Buenos Aires in 1954 and is one of Argentina's leading poets. She is the author of many books of poetry, including *El tapiz* (Tierra Baldía, 1983), *Cámara baja* (Último Reino, 1987), *La ópera fantasma* (Bajo la luna, 2005), *Las linternas flotantes* (Bajo la luna, 2009), *Diario ínfimo* (Isla de Siltolá, 2016), and *Glosa continua* (Editorial Excursiones, 2018). Translations of her work have been published in Italy, Quebec, Romania, France, England, and the United States. In the UK, Shearsman Books has published an anthology of her poetry, *Like the Rains Come* (2008), as well as her collection, *Floating Lanterns* (2016, translated by Anna Deeny). Translated by Judith Filc, her book, *Ghost Opera*, was published in the US in 2017 by co-im-press. She is the founder and editor of Ediciones Pen Press, a successful independent press dedicated to the publication of contemporary Spanish-language poets as well as poets of other languages in Spanish translation. Roffé has been the recipient of a John Simon Guggenheim Fellowship (2001) and a Civitella Ranieri Foundation Fellowship (2012).

Fabián Casas was born in the neighborhood of Boedo in Buenos Aires in 1965. He published the influential poetry journal *18 Whiskys* and was a leading figure of the Generación del 90, a movement characterized by colloquial speech, anti-lyricism, references to urban life and pop culture, and objectivism. Casas is the author of six books of poetry: *Tuca* (Libros de Tierra Firme, 1990), *El Salmón* (Libros de Tierra Firme, 1996), *Oda* (Libros de Tierra Firme, 2004), *El Spleen de Boedo* (Vox, 2005), *El hombre de overol* (Vox, 2006), and *Horla City y otros* (Emecé, 2010). In 2016, Eloísa Cartonera published his memoir, *Diarios de la Edad del Pavo*. Casas is also the author of two works of fiction: *Ocio* (Emecé, 2000) and *Los Lemmings y otros* (Santiago Arcos, 2005). With Lisandro Alonso, he wrote the screenplay for the surrealist Western, *Jauja*. In 2011, Casas was honored as one of the great Latin American writers of the 20th century at the Guadalajara International Book Fair. He is a brown belt in karate and currently works as a journalist.

Néstor Perlongher was born in 1949 in Avellanada, Buenos Aires Province, Argentina. Considered an instrumental figure of the Neobaroque movement in Argentina, his books of poetry include *Austria-Hungría* (Tierra Baldía, 1980), *Alambres* (Último Reino, 1987), *Hule* (Último Reino, 1989), *Parque Lezama* (Editorial Sudamericana, 1990), *Aguas Aéreas* (Último Reino, 1990), and *El chorreo de las iluminaciones* (La Pequeña Venecia, 1992). He received the Boris Vian Prize for *Alambres* in 1987, and in 1992, he was awarded a Guggenheim Fellowship. Perlongher was one of the founders of the Frente de Liberación Homosexual Argentino, and he was active in various movements against the violence committed by the military dictatorship. In 1981, he moved to São Paulo, where he studied Social Anthropology and taught as a professor at the State University of Campinas (UNICAM). In his work as an anthropologist, he focused on sex workers and gay and transgender subcultures. He died of AIDS in São Paulo in 1992.

Diana Bellessi was born in Zavalla, Santa Fe, in 1946, and is considered one of the most prominent poets to emerge in the years immediately following the dictatorship. She is the author of many books of poetry, including *Crucero equatorial* (1981), *Eróica* (1988), *El jardín* (1992), *La edad dorada* (2003), *La rebelión del instante* (2006), *Pasos de Baile* (2015), and *Fuerte como la muerte es el amor* (2018). A feminist poet, Bellessi was one of the founders of the influential *Revista Feminaria*, and she has translated the work of poets such as Denise Levertov, Adrienne Rich, and Ursula LeGuin. In 1993, she received a Guggenheim fellowship, and in 2004 and 2014 she received the Konex Award in Argentina.

ABOUT THE ARTIST

Alpe Romero was born in 1971 in Buenos Aires. Alpe's drawings are grounded in improvisation, the relationship between fiction and reality, and the ephemeral nature of time and movement. His work has appeared in exhibitions in Buenos Aires and Marseille, France, and his drawings were included in *Mañana Agua*, published by Random Ediciones in 2012. You can find him on Instagram at @romeroalpe.

ACKNOWLEDGEMENTS

I wish to express my appreciation to the editors of the following publications, where some of these poems and translations first appeared, often in different form: *Anomaly*, *Arts and Understanding*, *Asymptote*, *Aufgabe*, and *Ghost Proposal*.

Infinite thanks to Alejandro Méndez, Mercedes Roffé, Fabián Casas, and Diana Bellessi for their kindness and for trusting me with their beautiful poems. I am especially grateful to Roberto Echavarren for meeting me in Montevideo to talk about Néstor Perlongher, for giving me permission to translate his work, and for his many helpful insights.

I would also like to thank my friends in Buenos Aires, especially Alpe Romero, for the kinship we share and the wonderful drawings that accompany this book; to Fernando Caputo, for our long conversations about poetry, art, and politics; and to Matías Blanco, for making me feel at home. Many thanks to the wonderful people at Eloísa Cartonera, especially Miriam (Osa) Merlo, Alejandro Miranda, Ricardo Piña, and Washington Cucurto.

For helping me to think through the multiple iterations of this project and the intricacies of translation, I would like to thank Jen Hofer, Jen Scappettone, Constanza Svidler, Amina Cain, Joseph Gallucci, Benjamin Fife, Rae Gouirand, José Amador, and Megan Pruiett.

I am grateful to Pitzer College for providing research funding which made this project possible.

Finally, I would like to thank everyone at *The Operating System*, especially ELÆ [Lynne DeSilva-Johnson], for believing in this book and giving it a home. I'm deeply inspired by their commitment to innovative creative practice, translation and multilingual writing, community, and social transformation.

ABOUT THE AUTHOR / TRANSLATOR

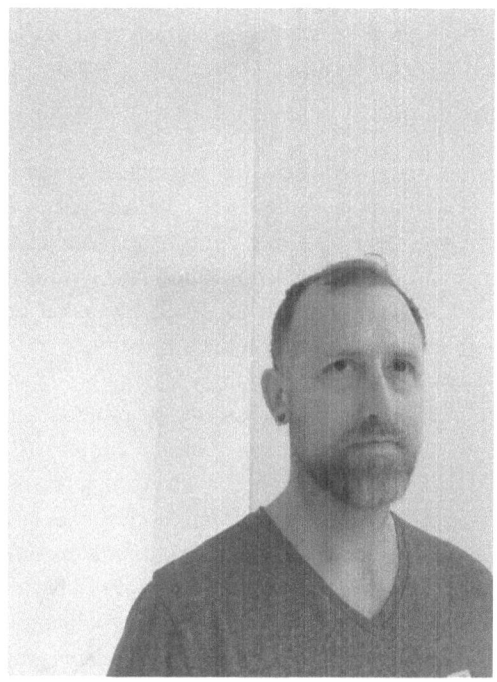

Brent Armendinger was born in Warsaw, NY, and studied at Bard College and the University of Michigan, where he received an Avery Hopwood Award in Poetry. In addition to *Street Gloss*, Brent is the author of *The Ghost in Us Was Multiplying* (Noemi Press, 2015), a finalist for the California Book Award in Poetry, and two chapbooks, *Undetectable* (New Michigan Press, 2009) and *Archipelago (Noemi Press, 2009)*. His poems and translations have appeared in many journals, including *Anomaly, Asymptote, Aufgabe, Bloom, Colorado Review, Denver Quarterly, Ghost Proposal, Hayden's Ferry Review, LIT, Puerto del Sol, Volt,* and *Web Conjunctions*. He is a recipient of residencies from Blue Mountain Center and Headlands Center for the Arts. Brent teaches creative writing at Pitzer College and lives in Los Angeles, where he is an active member of the L.A. Tenants Union.

GLOSSARIUM:UNSILENCED TEXTS

The Operating System's GLOSSARIUM: UNSILENCED TEXTS series was established in early 2016 in an effort to recover silenced voices outside and beyond the canon, seeking out and publishing both contemporary translations and little or un-known out of print texts, in particular those under siege by restrictive regimes and silencing practices in their home (or adoptive) countries. We are committed to producing dual-language versions whenever possible.

Few, even avid readers, are aware of the startling statistic reporting that less than three percent of all books published in the United States, per UNESCO, are works in translation. Less than one percent of these (closer to 0.7%) are works of poetry and fiction. You can imagine that even less of these are experiemental or radical works, in particular those from countries in conflict with the US or where funding is hard to come by.

Other countries are far, far ahead of us in reading and promoting international literature, a trend we should be both aware of and concerned about—how does it come to pass that our attentions become so myopic, and as a result, so under-informed? We see the publication of translations, especially in volume, to be a vital and necessary act for all publishers to require of themselves in the service of a more humane, globally aware, world. By publishing 7 titles in 2019, we stand to raise the number of translated books of literature published in the US this year *by a full percent*. We plan to continue this growth as much as possible.

The dual-language titles either in active circulation or forthcoming in this series include Arabic-English, Farsi-English, Polish-English, French-English, Faroese-English, Yaqui Indigenous American translations, and Spanish-English translations from Cuba, Argentina, Mexico, Uruguay, Bolivia, and Puerto Rico.

The term 'Glossarium' derives from latin/greek and is defined as 'a collection of glosses or explanations of words, especially of words not in general use, as those of a dialect, locality or an art or science, or of particular words used by an old or a foreign author.' The series is curated by OS Founder and Managing Editor Elæ [Lynne DeSilva-Johnson,] with the help of global collaborators and friends.

WHY PRINT / DOCUMENT?

The Operating System uses the language "print document" to differentiate from the book-object as part of our mission to distinguish the act of documentation-in-book-FORM from the act of publishing as a backwards-facing replication of the book's agentive *role* as it may have appeared the last several centuries of its history. Ultimately, I approach the book as TECHNOLOGY: one of a variety of printed documents (in this case, bound) that humans have invented and in turn used to archive and disseminate ideas, beliefs, stories, and other evidence of production.

Ownership and use of printing presses and access to (or restriction of printed materials) has long been a site of struggle, related in many ways to revolutionary activity and the fight for civil rights and free speech all over the world. While (in many countries) the contemporary quotidian landscape has indeed drastically shifted in its access to platforms for sharing information and in the widespread ability to "publish" digitally, even with extremely limited resources, the importance of publication on physical media has not diminished. In fact, this may be the most critical time in recent history for activist groups, artists, and others to insist upon learning, establishing, and encouraging personal and community documentation practices. Hear me out.

With The OS's print endeavors I wanted to open up a conversation about this: the ultimately radical, transgressive act of creating PRINT /DOCUMENTATION in the digital age. It's a question of the archive, and of history: who gets to tell the story, and what evidence of our life, our behaviors, our experiences are we leaving behind? We can know little to nothing about the future into which we're leaving an unprecedentedly digital document trail — but we can be assured that publications, government agencies, museums, schools, and other institutional powers that be will continue to leave BOTH a digital and print version of their production for the official record. Will we?

As a (rogue) anthropologist and long time academic, I can easily pull up many accounts about how lives, behaviors, experiences — how THE STORY of a time or place — was pieced together using the deep study of correspondence, notebooks, and other physical documents which are no longer the norm in many lives and practices. As we move our creative behaviors towards digital note taking, and even audio and video, what can we predict about future technology that is in any way assuring that our stories will be accurately told – or told at all? How will we leave these things for the record?

In these documents we say:
WE WERE HERE, WE EXISTED, WE HAVE A DIFFERENT STORY

- Elæ [Lynne DeSilva-Johnson], Founder/Creative Director
THE OPERATING SYSTEM, Brooklyn NY 2018

RECENT & FORTHCOMING FULL LENGTH
OS PRINT::DOCUMENTS and PROJECTS, 2018-19

2019

Y - Lori Anderson Moseman
Ark Hive-Marthe Reed
I Made for You a New Machine and All it Does is Hope - Richard Lucyshyn
Illusory Borders-Heidi Reszies
A Year of Misreading the Wildcats - Orchid Tierney
Collaborative Precarity Bodyhacking Work-book and Research Guide - stormy budwig, Elae [Lynne DeSilva-Johnson] and Cory Tamler
We Are Never The Victims - Timothy DuWhite
Of Color: Poets' Ways of Making | An Anthology of Essays on Transformative Poetics -Amanda Galvan Huynh & Luisa A. Igloria, Editors
The Suitcase Tree - Filip Marinovich
In Corpore Sano: Creative Practice and the Challenged* Body - Elae [Lynne DeSilva-Johnson] and Amanda Glassman, Editors

KIN(D)* TEXTS AND PROJECTS

A Bony Framework for the Tangible Universe-D. Allen
Opera on TV-James Lowell Brunton
Hall of Waters-Berry Grass
Transitional Object-Adrian Silbernagel

GLOSSARIUM: UNSILENCED TEXTS AND TRANSLATIONS

Śnienie / Dreaming - Marta Zelwan, (Poland, trans. Victoria Miluch)
Alparegho: Pareil-À-Rien / Alparegho, Like Nothing Else - Hélène Sanguinetti (France, trans. Ann Cefola)
High Tide Of The Eyes - Bijan Elahi (Farsi-English/dual-language)
trans. Rebecca Ruth Gould and Kayvan Tahmasebian
In the Drying Shed of Souls: Poetry from Cuba's Generation Zero
Katherine Hedeen and Víctor Rodríguez Núñez, translators/editors
Street Gloss - Brent Armendinger with translations for Alejandro Méndez, Mercedes Roffé, Fabián Casas, Diana Bellessi, and Néstor Perlongher (Argentina)
Operation on a Malignant Body - Sergio Loo (Mexico, trans. Will Stockton)
Are There Copper Pipes in Heaven - Katrin Ottarsdóttir
(Faroe Islands, trans. Matthew Landrum)

An Absence So Great and Spontaneous It Is Evidence of Light - Anne Gorrick
The Book of Everyday Instruction - Chloë Bass
Executive Orders Vol. II - a collaboration with the Organism for Poetic Research
One More Revolution - Andrea Mazzariello
Chlorosis - Michael Flatt and Derrick Mund
Sussuros a Mi Padre - Erick Sáenz
Abandoners - Lesley Ann Wheeler
Jazzercise is a Language - Gabriel Ojeda-Sague
Born Again - Ivy Johnson
Attendance - Rocío Carlos and Rachel McLeod Kaminer
Singing for Nothing - Wally Swist
Walking Away From Explosions in Slow Motion - Gregory Crosby
Field Guide to Autobiography - Melissa Eleftherion

KIN(D)* TEXTS AND PROJECTS

Sharing Plastic - Blake Nemec
The Ways of the Monster - Jay Besemer

GLOSSARIUM: UNSILENCED TEXTS AND TRANSLATIONS

The Book of Sounds - Mehdi Navid (Farsi dual language, trans. Tina Rahimi
Kawsay: The Flame of the Jungle - María Vázquez Valdez (Mexico, trans. Margaret Randall)
Return Trip / Viaje Al Regreso - Israel Dominguez; (Cuba, trans. Margaret Randall)

for our full catalog please visit:
https://squareup.com/store/the-operating-system/

deeply discounted Book of the Month and Chapbook Series subscriptions
are a great way to support the OS's projects and publications!
sign up at: http://www.theoperatingsystem.org/subscribe-join/

DOC U MENT
/däkyəmənt/

First meant "instruction" or "evidence," whether written or not.

noun - a piece of written, printed, or electronic matter that provides information or evidence or that serves as an official record
verb - record (something) in written, photographic, or other form
synonyms - paper - deed - record - writing - act - instrument

[*Middle English, precept, from Old French, from Latin documentum, example, proof, from docre, to teach; see dek- in Indo-European roots.*]

Who is responsible for the manufacture of value?

Based on what supercilious ontology have we landed in a space where we vie against other creative people in vain pursuit of the fleeting credibilities of the scarcity economy,
rather than
freely collaborating and sharing openly with each other in ecstatic celebration of MAKING?

While we understand and acknowledge the economic pressures and fear-mongering that threatens to dominate and crush the creative impulse, we also believe that
now more than ever we have the tools to relinquish agency via cooperative means,
fueled by the fires of the Open Source Movement.

Looking out across the invisible vistas of that rhizomatic parallel country we can begin to see our community beyond constraints, in the place where intention meets
resilient, proactive, collaborative organization.

Here is a document born of that belief, sown purely of imagination and will. When we document we assert. We print to make real, to reify our being there. When we do so with mindful intention to address our process, to open our work to others, to create beauty in words in space, to respect and acknowledge the strength of the page we now hold physical, a thing in our hand, we remind ourselves that, like Dorothy: *we had the power all along, my dears.*

THE PRINT! DOCUMENT SERIES
is a project of
the trouble with bartleby
in collaboration with
the operating system

www.ingramcontent.com/pod-product-compliance
Lightning Source LLC
Chambersburg PA
CBHW030120100526
44591CB00009B/472